CANADA
and the NEW AMERICAN EMPIRE

CANADA
and the **NEW AMERICAN EMPIRE**

WAR AND ANTI WAR

Edited by **GEORGE MELNYK**

©2004 George Melnyk
Published by the University of Calgary Press
2500 University Drive NW, Calgary,
Alberta, Canada T2N 1N4
www.uofcpress.com

We acknowledge the financial support of
the Government of Canada through the
Book Publishing Industry Development
Program (BPIDP) for our publishing
activities. We acknowledge the support of
the Alberta Foundation for the Arts for this
published work.

**National Library of Canada
Cataloguing in Publication**

Canada and the new American empire : war and
anti-war / edited by George Melnyk.

Includes bibliographical references.
ISBN 1-55238-130-7

1. Canada--Foreign relations--United States. 2.
United States--Foreign relations--Canada. 3. Iraq War,
2003. 4. War. 5. Peace. I. Melnyk, George

FC249.C322 2004   327.71073   C2004-900738-6

Canada

**Canada Council   Conseil des Arts
for the Arts   du Canada**

Printed and bound in Canada by
Houghton Boston

∞ This book is printed on 50% recycled,
acid-free paper

Cover design, page design and typesetting
by Mieka West. Production by Mike Stickel

To the people of Iraq in their search for peace,
democracy, justice and freedom

CONTENTS

ACKNOWLEDGMENTS

This book was initiated when the United States and the UK were landing troops in preparation for an invasion and occupation of Iraq, while millions around the world marched against the impending war. The book would not have been possible without the dedication of its contributors, who produced articles on short notice. I want to thank each of them for their efforts. Likewise, the energetic and speedy work of the staff of the University of Calgary Press is to be applauded. Walter Hildebrandt, director of the press, was committed to a book that would be accessible. Designer Mieka West brought her creative energies to the book with her usual enthusiasm and professional care.

I realize that I would not have been able to complete the project if I had not been on a sabbatical fellowship leave from teaching in the Faculty of Communication and Culture during the first half of 2003. I am most grateful for this opportunity. This book was a last-minute decision that I added to other scholarly book-writing projects I was already engaged in. This project overburdened an already stretched capacity. I would like to extend a very special appreciation to my wife Julia who helped me emotionally and editorially. Without her help my juggling act would have collapsed.

Finally, I would like to thank the Board of Directors of the Dr. Irma M. Parhad Fund at the University of Calgary for their decision to assist financially with the publication of this book.

INTRODUCTION

FROM WAR TO PEACE

George Melnyk

An American bomb cloud
in full sunlight
rises from a green
hill bunker horizon
dark density roiling
and lifting
a towering deity
with ears of Mickey Mouse
swelling and shifting
against blue sky[1]

Ivan Sundal

The friendly image of a larger-than-life Mickey Mouse has turned into the deadly image of a vaporizing bomb cloud during the last two years because of the American invasion and occupation of Afghanistan and Iraq. Iraq has the second largest confirmed reserves of oil in the world after Saudi Arabia. The United States is the largest consumer of oil in the world. Not only does Iraq have an enormous storehouse of oil, it also has the "cheapest production costs in the world, at about a dollar a barrel."[2] This cost of production is one-sixth of production costs in the United States. With Saudi Arabia firmly in the U.S. camp, an independently minded state with grandiose plans like Iraq under Saddam Hussain posed a threat to U.S. geopolitical ambitions in the region. With Texas oil interests deeply embedded in the current Bush administration, what could be viewed theoretically as a match made in heaven has turned into a reality made in hell.

There are four key concepts in the title of this book. The first is "Canada," the second is the "new American empire," the third is "war" and the fourth is "anti-war." The United States and war are one link, while Canada and anti-war is the second link. Ever since September 11th, 2001, when the World Trade Center in New York and the Pentagon in Washington were attacked, there has been a major struggle to win over Canadian public sentiment to either a pro-war or an anti-war position.[3] The pro-war side has painted its position as one of unfettered friendliness to the United States and support for its global campaign against its enemies. In the past two years, the United States has invaded and occupied two countries – Afghanistan and Iraq – one with the support and involvement of Canada and the other without. Imperialism works through military occupation, and it is today's unrivalled American military strength that is fuelling the new imperialism. The question is what is Canada's role in this new imperialism and what are the consequences of involvement or non-involvement in war for Canadian society?

This book is an examination of this contentious issue from the perspective of the anti-war side of the debate. When Iraq was under attack and the world displayed a near-unanimous condemnation of the invasion and its justification, anti-war sentiment was global and very loud. For example, more than 200,000 Montrealers marched against the war in March 2003. Even in the right-wing, pro-American oil centre of Calgary over five thousand citizens marched in the largest anti-war demonstration that city had ever seen. This outpouring of anti-war sentiment was unable to stop the invasion. Opposition from major European allies, especially France, and from a ringing chorus of foreign governments was unable to stop the invasion. With the U.S. and British invasion and occupation a *fait accompli* and the United States trying to drag the UN into recreating Iraq in a manner suited to the United States, the tone of global opposition has softened as various governments position themselves around the energy banquet table and seek a return to "normal" relations with the U.S. superpower. The establishment media suggests that the new prime minister, Paul Martin, will turn Canada into a staunch ally of the U.S. war machine, unlike Jean Chrétien, his predecessor.[4]

There is little likelihood that future invasions of small weak states by the United States can or will be stopped. After the Iraq experience, when most of the world stood against the United States and yet failed to stop the invasion, Canadians should not be asking themselves how the United States can be prevented from continued imperialist expansion and its now-realized ambition of global hegemony. Instead, Canadians should be asking themselves how Canada can remove itself from the imperial equation by embracing the anti-war side.

When Canada refused to join the United States and Great Britain in its falsely justified aggression, Canada stood with the world community in voicing opposition to what has become the new imperial world order of the twenty-first century. After the collapse of the Soviet Union in 1991, the United States became the world's sole hyperpower, and with that power came a renewed U.S. military aggressiveness that went far beyond the usual machinations of the Cold War (exceeded only in Vietnam) or the geographic limits of the Monroe Doctrine, in which Central and South America were U.S. fiefdoms. Other than Europe (an ally) and the two regional powers of Russia and China with their limited spheres of influence, the world remains open to unilateral U.S. control and, if necessary, occupation.

Canada has not been shy about supporting the United States in its military campaigns ever since 1991, when it participated in the Gulf War. This was followed by the use of Canadian airpower against Yugoslavia in 1999 and the use of ground troops in Afghanistan in 2001–2003 in support of American objectives. In the 1990s Canada was part of the new militarism, whether under the guise of Security Council approval or as a member of NATO, and it continues to be a military adjunct of U.S. ambitions in a very real and costly way to the Canadian taxpayer. This is particularly true of Afghanistan, where Canada is supplying several thousand occupying troops (termed "peacekeepers") under the banner of the NATO-led International Security Assistance Force.[5] The refusal to participate in the invasion of Iraq was a departure from this basic thrust. The implications of that refusal and how it came about and what the refusal means for Canada's future is the core of the fifteen essays presented in this book. The authors, who come from a variety of backgrounds – academic, activist, and political – speak out of a Canadian experience and understanding that is still very much in process as the new American empire unfolds before us. The authors support the peace option for Canada over the war option, and they explore the ways in which Canada can maintain an independent foreign policy in the midst of an unparalleled push for imperial power.

The push for empire is cloaked in the reactionary, U.S.-originated "clash of civilizations" argument that claims that Islam, especially in the Middle East, is the enemy of the West and must be subjugated because it is a threat.[6] Just as godless communism was the monstrous other of the Cold War for U.S. capitalism, so now a new religious and ideological enemy has been created to replace the former. The new fear of "terrorists" (read Arabs) has replaced the old fear of "communists," but it is the same old fear-mongering. The "us versus them" universe created by war, scape-goating, and political lies such as those that justified the invasion of Iraq (supposed weapons of mass destruction and links to terrorism), none of which have been shown to be true, is precisely the universe that the authors in this collection oppose.[7] They want Canada to play a role in helping the Iraqi people in their search for peace, democracy, justice, and freedom from occupation.

The book is divided into three main sections and an afterword. The first section is titled "Thinking" and is meant to allow readers to gain a critical perspective on the history of Canadian, American, and Iraqi relations. The first essay by Douglas Roche, a senior Canadian parliamentarian, long-time peace activist and foreign development critic, and author of numerous books on international issues, outlines in a clear and forceful manner the choice that Canada needs to make if it is to maintain an unbiased international presence. Next, the role of the Canadian and North American media in creating the Middle Eastern "Other" is explored with chilling insight by Tareq and Jacqueline Ismael of the University of Calgary. These scholars identify the anti-Muslim bias of the media as one of the major stumbling blocks to peace. Philosopher Trudy Govier of Calgary, the author of a best-selling text on critical thinking, a work on social trust, and most recently a critical look at the events of September 11 (*A Delicate Balance: What Philosophy Can Tell Us About Terrorism*) exposes the lack of logic at the core of the arguments used to bolster violence as an appealing solution to international conflict. Liberal member of Parliament Colleen Beaumier and her assistant Joyce Patel provide a detailed history of the humanitarian crisis caused by a decade of UN sanctions, which helped to devastate the

Iraqi economy and impoverish its once prosperous people. The section concludes with an analysis by University of Regina adjunct professor of human justice Jim Harding, who takes a long, hard look at the ideological underpinnings of the new American empire and what the Bush Doctrine of U.S. military invincibility means for Canada.

The second section, titled "Acting," provides perspectives by those actively involved in opposing the war on Iraq. It documents their peace activism, beginning with Dr. David Swann of Calgary, who offers an autobiographical account of his fact-finding trip to Iraq in 2002, just prior to the invasion. His moving account is followed by the passionate voice of the Very Reverend Bill Phipps, former moderator of the United Church of Canada, who presents his reflections on how faith stands in the forefront of global peace activism. Donn Lovett provides a fascinating insight on how one very ordinary Canadian citizen was able to move diplomatic mountains to further the peace option. He also explains what he and others are trying to accomplish in Iraq today by creating institutions of civil society. Dr. Arthur Clark of the Department of Clinical Neuo-sciences at the University of Calgary and founder of the Dr. Irma M. Parhad Programmes for peace and international understanding at the University of Calgary makes a lucid argument for greater individual citizen responsibility in opposing war and upholding international law. Dr. Robert Hackett of Simon Fraser University is a scholar on media and democracy and former co-director of NewsWatch Canada. His essay outlines the basic corporatist structure of North American media and suggests strategies for finding alternative news sources that provide counter-establishment perspectives on peace and democracy. The section concludes with Canadian studies professor George Melnyk's argument that the United States has created a paradigm of endless war in which it seeks and expects Canadian complicity. He concludes his essay with a call for a Canadian boycott of U.S. products, services, and visits in order to help wean Canadians from their dependence on the United States.

The final section, titled "Observing," offers three international perspectives on the Canadian dilemma of peace versus war. The section begins with former U.S. Marine Scott Ritter's account of his experiences as the UN's chief weapons inspector in Iraq during the 1990s and his view of Canada's role in the inspection process. Ritter is best known for his 1999 book *Endgame: Solving the Iraq Crisis*, which was followed by *War with Iraq: What Team Bush Doesn't Want you to Know* (2000). His insider's account raises questions about Canada's commitment to its peacekeeping role in the inspection process. His essay is followed by a comparison of Mexico and Canada's reaction to war and invasion. The refusal of both countries to participate suggests to Dr. Hussain, professor of international studies at the Universidad Iberoamericana in Mexico City, that there may be increasing grounds for Mexican/Canadian cooperation in international affairs. Dr. Satya Pattnayak, associate professor of sociology and director of Latin American studies at Villanova University, sees the unilateral approach of the United States as unrivalled from an international balance of power perspective. He discusses how this reality limits Canada's desire for seeking solutions to international conflict through a multilateral approach.

The final word belongs to Mel Hurtig, a prominent Canadian nationalist, who provides an epilogue for the book. He points out how the economic imperatives of NAFTA, the Bush administration and its representatives, the continentalist interests of Canada's business elite, the uncritically pro-American Canadian media and the Official Opposition have come together to wage war on an independent foreign policy for Canada. Unless the economic knot that ties Canada to the United States is loosened, he argues, the pro-American war editorializing of these sectors will continue to restrict Canada's commitment to multilaterialism in international affairs.

The American and British occupation of Iraq and its appointment of a puppet government has been revealed as simple, old-fashioned imperialism. For example, the U.S.-appointed Iraqi Governing Council has announced that it was opening up the country to foreign investment by privatizing the whole of the state-owned Iraqi economy, other than oil.[8] The announcement was described as " a free-market economic laboratory, with levels of foreign ownership and privatization never before seen in the Arab world." [9] The privatization is being engineered by a U.S. firm that received a $US80 million contract to do the work. Privatization includes the foreign ownership of Iraq's national banks, a move welcomed by the International Monetary Fund and the World Bank, key agents of U.S. capitalist expansionism.[10] Meanwhile, life for the people of Iraq remains oppressive, chaotic, arbitrary and unpredictable, and very dangerous.

Because of Canada's intense economic ties to the United States and its continued participation in international entities like U.S.-dominated NATO, the pursuit of a peace option in an era of increased U.S. aggression is a profound and disturbing challenge for Canadians who oppose war. And there are more war clouds on the horizon. The U.S. paradigm of endless war, growing out of its unchallenged military domination, point to more U.S.-initiated wars in the future. The cost in human lives and national infrastructures will continue to grow as U.S. missiles, bombs, bullets, and artillery shells rain down on innocent women and children and poorly armed opponents. A U.S. peace activist who served as a "human shield" in Iraq during the American invasion remembered her week as a volunteer in a Baghdad hospital after the bombing had stopped:

It's just sobbing doctors, because there was so much death, so much horror.... It was just death after death after

death. From babies to old men and women, the whole
range. Amputees. Arms gone, legs gone. Children filled
with shrapnel from cluster bombs.[11]

If this is the scenario from one relatively short invasion, the outlines of a new imperialism involving many wars is truly frightening. The peace option is now needed more than ever, and its promotion as a cornerstone of Canadian foreign policy is something that will require the hard work, dedication, and humility of many Canadians.

I leave my readers with two images. The first is a CTV news broadcast on 8 November 2003 that showed American soldiers placing plastic bags over the heads of suspected insurgents so they could not see and could barely breathe. This kind of action by occupying forces, once condemned, is now considered normal and does not even raise an outcry. The second image is of a pile of books in a remaindered section of an independent bookstore at about the same time as the television broadcast. The book was published earlier in 2003 and contained poems by Canadian writers opposed to the war. The books were being sold at a deep discount. It is so easy to forget, to turn to other matters, to get on with our lives. In his foreword to *The Common Sky*, Alistair MacLeod wrote: "Throughout recorded history, it has often been the responsibility of the writer to speak out against the monstrosity of war."[12] The contributors to this book, like the poets, have responded by taking their responsibility for peace seriously. Let us hope many Canadians will continue to participate in this noble, but difficult struggle.

Notes

1 Poem published with the permission of the author.

2 John Cassidy, "Beneath the Sand," *The New Yorker* (14 and 16 July 2003): 66.

3 See Karim-Aly Kassam, George Melnyk, Lynne Perras, eds. *Canada and September 11: Impact and Response* (Calgary: Detselig, 2001) for a collection of essays on Canadian perspectives on September 11th.

4 One small example is a story on the Pentagon's Richard Perle, a leading proponent of the new imperialism, who commented negatively on the Chrétien legacy. See Drew Fagan, "Leading Bush advisor criticizes Chrétien's failure to help U.S.," *The Globe and Mail* (25 September 2003): A1.

5 Matthew Fisher, "Canadian general to lead peacekeeping efforts," *Calgary Herald* (27 September 2003): A4.

6 To see how this plays out in the Middle East see the interview with the Pakistani dictator, General Pervez Musharraf in *The Globe and Mail* (26 September 2003): A15, in which he says: "There is a general feeling that maybe the Muslim world or the religion of Islam is being targeted by Western governments.... While the perception in the West is the opposite, that Islam as a religion is a religion of extremism, terrorism, fundamentalism, intolerance."

7 In a far-reaching review of the bogus arguments put forward by Bush's ally, Tony Blair, and an analysis of American imperialist ambitions, Michael Meacher, the UK's environment minister from May 1997 to June 2003, concludes that the United States and the United Kingdom created "a political myth ... to pave the way for ... the U.S. goal of world hegemony, built around securing by force command over the oil supplies required to drive the whole project."

8 Doug Saunders, "Bagdad opens door to free market," *The Globe and Mail* (22 September 2003): A1, A9.

9 Ibid.

10 Ibid., A9.

11 Jennifer Frey, " A Human Shield's Undying Memories of Iraq," *Calgary Herald* (17 May 2003): OS1.

12 Alistair MacLeod, "Foreword," in *The Common Sky: Canadian Writers Against the War* (Toronto: Three Squares Press, 2003), p. vii.

THINKING: CANADA'S INVOLVEMENT IN AMERICAN WARS

THE U.S. OR THE UN:
A CHOICE FOR CANADA

Senator Douglas Roche

On 19 March 2003, U.S. President Al Gore called together his National Security officials to decide whether war would be necessary in Iraq to cleanse the country of weapons of mass destruction. U.S. forces, deployed in Kuwait and offshore, were poised to attack. The UN Security Council was in almost continuous session. The latest reports of the UN inspection team, headed by Hans Blix and Mohammed elBaradei, were being scrutinized. Russia, France, Germany, and China, all heavyweights in the Security Council, were insisting that the inspection process — though rebuffed at first by Saddam Hussein — was working. Eighty-four professional inspectors had conducted 500 inspections at 350 sites in Iraq and turned up no evidence of weapons of mass destruction. Six smaller states on the Security Council, Mexico, Chile, Pakistan, Guinea, Cameroon, and Angola, were sending signals to Washington to show restraint and give the inspection process more time. Pentagon officials warned that the decision on whether to go to war could not be deferred any longer.

President Gore looked around the room before speaking. All eyes were on him. "If the Security Council will not authorize military action, the United States will not strike," he said. "But we will insist that the UN double the number of inspectors in Iraq. We will comb every square inch of the country." The augmented inspection process continued for another month. No weapons of mass destruction or any facilities to produce them were found, but the Security Council decided to leave inspectors inside Iraq for the next several years. The United States stood down its forces.

"Rather than spending money on war, let's put more money into all the UN processes," President Gore told his cabinet shortly after the Iraq crisis. "Let's show the world the United States wants to strengthen the rule of law." In quick order, the U.S. Senate ratified the Comprehensive Test Ban Treaty and the Kyoto Protocol on the environment. The Gore Administration signed onto the International Criminal Court and pledged that it would never put weapons of any kind in space. President Gore himself instructed his arms control and disarmament negotiators to fly to Moscow, London, Paris, and Beijing to press the other Nuclear Weapons States to commence immediate negotiations on a ten-year plan for the complete elimination of nuclear weapons.

The President found time for a one-day visit to Ottawa. The Prime Minister escorted Gore into a cheering House of Commons. "Thank you, Canada," President Gore said as he began his speech. "Your constant work to shore up the United Nations as the most important instrument for peace in the world, your professional scientific and political work for verification methods, your unwavering commitment to the use of your armed forces for peace-building have been an inspiration to the people of the United States and indeed the world. Canada is the kind of neighbour the United States cherishes." The parliamentar-

ians were on their feet, yelling "Gore, Gore, Gore!" Svend Robinson, M.P., darted from his seat to present the U.S. President with a red rose....

Zzzttt!

That abrupt sound you just heard was my alarm clock going off. Rudely awakened, my dream shattered, I got up to face another day in the cold, real world of politics. The United States was cheering President George W. Bush (it was Bush, after all, not Al Gore, who emerged from the Florida debacle with a U.S. Supreme Court-backed claim to the presidency) for having liberated Iraq from the demonized Saddam Hussein. Kofi Annan was expediting humanitarian aid to Iraq and struggling to have the UN play a central role in the reconstruction of the country. "The feeling of global insecurity has seldom, if ever, been greater than it is today," he told the Security Council. "We are clearly at a crucial juncture in the development of international relations." The Arab world, relieved that Saddam Hussein was gone, wondered if the United States would strike again.

In Canada, two back-to-back debates took place in the House of Commons: one, on a motion sponsored by the Canadian Alliance, calling on the House of Commons to apologize to the United States for offensive comments made by some of its members and to reaffirm that the United States is "Canada's closest friend and ally," and the other, on a motion sponsored by the government, reaffirming the government's decision not to participate in the Iraq war, and restating "the unbreakable bonds of values, family, friendship and mutual respect that will always characterize Canada's relationship with the United States...."

It is a hallmark of Canada's obsession with Canada–U.S. relations that, at the very moment the world is agitated with the United States for trampling on international political and legal systems, Parliament is focusing on not hurting U.S.

feelings. Unbreakable bond or not, Bush cancelled his planned visit to Ottawa.

The UN or the U.S.

The world is at a turning point in history, brought on by the United States and its assertion that a pre-emptive attack on Iraq in order to change the leadership regime was justified. This sea-change in international relations, for this is what it is when the world's most powerful state adopts a policy to depose governments it finds unfavourable, has opened a void that will be filled by one of two scenarios: either the world will be run by international law, centring in the UN system, or it will be run by the United States, by far the strongest military power ever seen.

Let it be said at the outset that the Government of Canada did the right thing when Prime Minister Jean Chrétien stood up in the House of Commons two days before the U.S. and U.K.-led coalition launched its attack on Iraq, and said: "If military action proceeds without a new resolution of the Security Council, Canada will not participate." Eight months earlier, the Department of Foreign Affairs and International Trade had crafted a memo, which Foreign Affairs Minister Bill Graham took to Cabinet. The memo foresaw that the Bush Administration was determined to oust Saddam Hussein with or without United Nations' approval. Whether the UN inspection process, resumed after Resolution 1441 was adopted, found anything or not, the United States was going to war. The memo recommended that, absent UN authorization, Canada stay out of the war. Prime Minister Chrétien had no trouble with this advice. Skeptical of U.S. intentions, but wary of giving offence to a trading partner that is like an elephant in the Canadian living room, Chrétien accepted the memo.

Nor did he have much trouble with his Cabinet, although the embassy in Washington was warning of dire consequences if Canada did not support the United States.

But Chrétien then made a mistake. He thought that, although it threatened war, the United States would not actually launch an attack without any evidence of Iraq producing weapons of mass destruction. Chrétien's logic led him to believe he could finesse Canada's public position so that it would never have to actually say no to the United States. A full-fledged communications strategy, making clear the reasons for Canada's principled position, was never invoked. When the final hours loomed and Chrétien realized the United States was indeed going to war, he quickly put together a short statement that he used to answer the lead question in Question Period.

Public opinion in Canada at first gave substantial support to the prime minister's position. But as the war progressed, a rally-round-the-troops feeling took hold in Canada, mirroring increased support for the war in the United States and the United Kingdom. On White House orders, U.S. Ambassador to Canada Paul Cellucci publicly complained about Canada's demurral, and then it became known that Canada had some thirty armed forces personnel serving on an exchange basis with U.S. and UK forces who were caught up in combat operations, even if from a distance. Suddenly, the Canadian stand did not look so principled. And when a few members of the Liberal government made none-too-flattering comments about U.S. leadership (Bush was called a "moron" and a "failed statesman," and Americans were damned as "bastards"), the right-wing press in Canada turned on Chrétien for damaging Canada's pre-eminent international relationship. Canada–U.S. relations were wrecked, they intoned. Chrétien did his usual dance in Parliament – and now the Canada–U.S. relationship has once again become the preoccupation of Canadian foreign policy.

The Pitfalls of Unilateralism

While Chrétien has been hard-pressed to stave off domestic attacks on his reluctance to fall in line behind U.S. policy in Iraq, the fallout from the American invasion, which is turning out to be a crash-course for the Pentagon in peace-building, is showing the wisdom of his position more and more. Though the U.S. military has proven very effective in toppling Saddam from power and winning the war, faced with a devastated Iraqi infrastructure as a result of the much celebrated "shock and awe" campaign, a lack of functioning state institutions, and a colossal power vacuum created by the exit of the all-powerful Baath party, it has been markedly less successful in winning the peace. In confronting all these challenges, the military has also been faced with an ongoing guerrilla campaign conducted by Saddam loyalists and others that has resulted in an ongoing string of American casualties.

Faced with falling troop morale and increased costs of occupation estimated at $4 billion per month (double initial projections), the United States has been forced to reach out to the international community for help. However, traditional U.S. allies have been reluctant to commit money or troops so long as the United States refuses to cede additional authority to the UN. (While the UN was given a supporting role under Security Council Resolution 1483, passed in May, 2003, the U.S.-led coalition retained responsibility for security and for the administration of reconstruction contracts.) International calls for a stronger UN role have been echoed by prominent Iraqi civilians, who argue that its neutrality gives the UN added legitimacy.

In his customarily wise and calm manner, Kofi Annan sized up the dilemma the United States found itself in:

> I think that the message that comes through loud and clear, given reactions of other Member States, is that multilateralism is important for many States around the world, that for many States the United Nations is important, that the imprimatur of the United Nations – the legitimacy the United Nations offers – is important. I think that this is a very clear message, particularly for those who thought that the United Nations was dead and had no influence. I must admit to you that I did warn those who were bashing the United Nations that they had to be careful, because they might need the United Nations soon.[1]

Canada–U.S. relations in the aftermath of the U.S. invasion of Iraq reflect Canada's perceived need to continue to support the primary role of the UN in authorizing the use of force to settle disputes, while at the same time avoiding antagonizing the Bush administration and risking devastating economic consequences. Immediately following the launch of the invasion of Iraq, Washington said it was "disappointed" with Canada's refusal to participate. Facing ongoing trade disputes with the United States over softwood lumber, the mad cow crisis, and a steep decline in summer tourism revenues over the outbreak of SARS in Toronto, Chrétien carefully avoided criticizing American policy in Iraq.

There is clearly a growing concern among Canadians about the direction of U.S. foreign policy. Polls revealed in June 2003 that only 63 per cent of Canadians viewed the United States favourably, down from 72 per cent a year earlier. The feeling was mutual, as the percentage of Americans who viewed Canada favourably dropped to 65 per cent from 85 per cent in 2002. Hostility towards the United States rose even more dramatically in other states, particularly in the Muslim world. Growing concerns about the validity of U.S. and British intelligence on Iraq's WMD programs have only fuelled this growing resentment toward the United States, and Bush and UK Prime Minister Tony Blair faced calls for a comprehensive investigation into charges that they may have deliberately manipulated information to justify war.

While other states have cited the need for a further UN resolution before peacekeepers can be sent, Canada's reluctance appears to be at least in part the result of an over-extended military, strained to its limits by the deployment of a large force to Afghanistan in the summer of 2003. To show its support for the United States (and the Iraqi people), Canada has committed some $100 million to aid in the reconstruction of Iraq. Furthermore, concern over relations with the Bush administration led the government on 30 May 2003, to agree to begin negotiating its participation in the U.S. missile defence program. This came after putting off formal consultations for years amid concerns that the program could destabilize international security, in part by leading to the weaponization of space.

The handling of the Iraq war has clearly knocked Canada off balance in its longstanding juggling act trying to keep the U.S. and UN balls in the air at the same time. This juggling act is known in the trade as the internationalists vs. the continentalists. They are struggling anew for control of Canadian foreign policy. The UN route or the U.S. route? Which shall Canada follow? The question is not new, but the circumstances are, since U.S. dominance now threatens to emasculate the UN, which for Canada has always been a prime outlet for its foreign policy.

The 'Balance' Strategy

There are many memoirs and analyses of the Canada–U.S. relationship emphasizing the historical difficulty for Canada to maintain a distinct foreign policy while living beside an economic giant which, given the chance, would smother Canada in a benign embrace. The cross-border disputes over fish, beef, lumber, wheat, and a host of commodities are legion. Canada's economic and environmental dependence on U.S. good will toward us is certainly not new, as the long dispute over acid rain illustrated. The good will was substantially drawn upon in getting the U.S. Senate to agree to "fast track" negotiations for the Free Trade Agreement – which otherwise reluctant senators agreed to because Canada had agreed to test U.S. cruise missile delivery systems over its territory. The increasing integration of the two countries' defence industries, making Canada unduly dependent on U.S. technology and equipment and the policy decisions that underpin this production, also illustrates the integral relationship.

U.S. administrations made it very clear throughout the Cold War that they expected Canada's support on security policies. Canada allowed cruise missile testing, softened its call for a nuclear test ban, and supported the U.S. invasion of Grenada and Panama, not out of conviction, but because of U.S. determination. Prime Minister Trudeau's 1983 peace initiative was doomed from the start through the derision of U.S. officials. U.S. antipathy to new approaches to human security has continued to constrain what should otherwise be Canadian promotion of the kind of international security regime that Canadian values have long espoused.

Canada supported its neighbour in 1991, when the United States pushed the UN Security Council into authorizing military action against Iraq. When, without a UN mandate, the U.S.-led NATO bombed Serbia and Kosovo in 1999, Canada played the faithful ally. So Canada is not above sublimating its UN values. But when the second Iraq war loomed, ostensibly over the issue of inspections but in reality to depose Saddam Hussein, Canada balked. No specific UN mandate, no war for Canada.

The "balance" strategy is embedded in Canadian foreign policy. The 1995 document, *Canada in the World*, spells it out:

> *The Government agrees that Canada intensify its efforts to advance the global disarmament and non-proliferation regime.... The United Nations continues to be the key vehicle for pursuing Canada's global security objectives.... As an active member of NATO and a net contributor to overall Alliance Security, as a friend and neighbour of the United States and its partner in NORAD ... Canada balances its Alliance obligations with its disarmament and non-proliferation goals.[2]*

The "balance" argument presupposes that the United States will at least stay on an even keel. But the Bush Administration has plunged the United States into a new era in which domination is its clear goal. This domination is, of course, marketed as the route to peace for the world. The peace foreseen by the hard-right ideologues driving the Bush agenda is based on overwhelming military and economic power. This is the very kind of "Pax Americana" that President John F. Kennedy warned the American people against in 1963. But because the Bush Administration has been able to sell at least some of the world on the idea that the UN cannot keep the peace, the United States has presented itself as the new saviour.

U.S. Policy on Nuclear Weapons

The National Security Strategy, which calls for pre-emptive attack against an opponent the U.S. Administration deems threatening, and the Nuclear Posture Review, which asserts that nuclear weapons will remain the cornerstone of U.S. military doctrine, have turned upside down both the nuclear non-proliferation regime and the very processes of international law.

The United States may still be a member of the United Nations, but it has turned its back on the multilateral world body. The Bush Administration has contempt for the UN. This ugly trait reveals itself in many global security issues but none more so than in the thorny questions surrounding the future of nuclear weapons.

The promises the United States made when the Non-Proliferation Treaty was indefinitely extended in 1995 – to participate actively in the total elimination of nuclear weapons – have become worthless. Under the guise of nuclear disarmament initiatives made in the Moscow Treaty of 2002, the United States is retaining huge stocks, developing a new nuclear weapon, deflecting criticism for rejecting the Comprehensive Test Ban Treaty, and rushing ahead with the development of a missile defence system, which many experts argue can only lead to the weaponization of space. The Nuclear Posture Review establishes expansive plans to revitalize U.S. nuclear forces, and all the systems and doctrines that support them, within a New Triad of capabilities that combine nuclear and conventional offensive strikes with missile defences and nuclear weapons infrastructure. The NPR assumes that nuclear weapons will be part of U.S. forces for at least the next fifty years. Ten U.S. senators, led by Senator Edward M. Kennedy of Massachusetts, have expressed "grave concern" about the widened U.S. rationale for the use of nuclear weapons.

Faced with a constantly modernizing U.S. nuclear arsenal and new high tech systems of which missile defences are only one part, existing nuclear weapons states are likely to retain their nuclear stocks. And more states, seeing that nuclear weapons are the true currency of power, may follow India, Pakistan, and Israel's recourse to acquiring nuclear weapons. The controversy over North Korea's missile testing shows how precarious the non-proliferation regime is. The danger of a nuclear catastrophe grows.

That catastrophe may well be set off by terrorists. Immediately after September 11, UN Secretary-General Kofi Annan went to Ground Zero in New York and said that, as horrible as the destruction was, it would have been much worse had the terrorists used nuclear devices. He called on nations to "re-double" efforts to implement fully the relevant treaties to stop the spread of nuclear and other weapons of mass destruction.

It is the lack of an enforceable convention to shut off the development and production of nuclear weapons and fissile materials that has resulted in the new risk of nuclear terrorism. There has been resolution after resolution at the UN for a Nuclear Weapons Convention; the resolutions actually pass with handsome majorities (although Canada has never voted in favour). Public opinion polls throughout the world show that people heavily favour the abolition of all nuclear weapons. But the United States and the other nuclear weapons states refuse to enter such negotiations, so determined are they to preserve their nuclear power. Now the world faces not only the traditional prospect of a nuclear war between states but the use of a nuclear weapon by terrorists who steal, or are given, nuclear materials. In this new age of suicidal mass terrorism, the threat of attacks using weapons of mass destruction has grown exponentially. Virtually all experts on the subject say it is not a question of whether a massive attack will occur, but when.

The new U.S. policies have brought the world to a new moment regarding nuclear weapons. In fact, the United States has introduced the world to the Second Nuclear Age, and Russia is following quickly on U.S. heels. Instead of progress towards elimination, we are seeing the dismantling of the non-proliferation regime, constructed so laboriously over the past three decades. NATO is caught up in this dismantling. And so is Canada.

Canada's Nuclear Ambiguity

Foreign Minister Bill Graham is well aware of this new dilemma. It was Graham, after all, who chaired the Parliamentary Committee that, in 1998, recommended that Canada press NATO to review its nuclear policies. A review was started but it came to naught. Six NATO countries, Belgium, Greece, The Netherlands, Germany, Italy, and Turkey, which are classified as non-nuclear, actually have a total of 180 tactical U.S. nuclear weapons stationed on their soil. When the New Agenda Coalition[3] submitted a resolution to the UN in 2002 calling for these tactical nuclear weapons to be included as an integral part of the nuclear arms reduction and disarmament process, Canada abstained. However, in a courageous move, Graham authorized a yes vote on a New Agenda omnibus resolution, which reaffirmed the Thirteen Practical Steps for nuclear disarmament adopted at the NPT 2000 Review. Canada was the only NATO country to vote in favour of the new resolution.

Canada would like to see the world rid itself of nuclear weapons. There is no doubt of that. But the government allows itself to remain in an incoherent posture: wearing its NPT hat, Canada subscribes to the elimination of nuclear weapons; wearing its NATO hat, Canada stays loyal to NATO's insistence on the retention of nuclear weapons. The contradiction of Canada's nuclear weapons policies going in two opposite directions at the same time is the direct result of Canada's subservience to U.S. nuclear polices. This ambiguity was clearly depicted by Project Ploughshares, a leading analytical NGO, which said:

> *Nearly sixty years after the advent of the nuclear age, Canada still maintains a fundamentally ambiguous policy toward nuclear weapons. The Canadian government rules out acquiring its own nuclear weapons, opposes nuclear proliferation, and asserts that "the only sustainable strategy for the future is the elimination of nuclear weapons entirely." But it also supports the continued possession of nuclear weapons by its allies, participates in a nuclear-armed alliance, and endorses NATO's plan to retain nuclear weapons "for the foreseeable future." The Canadian government continues to state that the defence of Canada must rely on the "nuclear umbrella" that the United States and other NATO allies have unfurled above this country, and it continues to provide both physical and political support for those weapons in a variety of ways. In short, while the Canadian government condemns any reliance on nuclear weapons by non-allied countries, it continues to treat those same weapons as a useful – even necessary – element of Canada's defences and those of its allies.*[4]

Now, as a result of U.S. policies, the Non-Proliferation Treaty – the centrepiece of Canadian policy – is unravelling. A policy that was justified as "balanced" is now facilitating the collapse of the NPT and the undermining of the UN. Each day, the warning of the Canberra Commission, organized a few years ago by the Government of Australia, rings more true: "The possession of nuclear weapons by any state is a constant stimulus to others to acquire them." Jayantha Dhanapala, former UN Under-Secretary-General for Disarmament Affairs, calls the gulf between declarations and deeds in nuclear disarmament "alarming."

In this suddenly more perilous international system, what can Canada do?

A New International Initiative

The Canadian Pugwash Group, the Canadian branch of the international Pugwash movement, which won the 1995 Nobel Peace Prize for its work on nuclear disarmament, has recommended that Canada launch what would be the nuclear equivalent of the "Ottawa Process" on landmines. Just as the initiative of the Government of Canada, in calling for an international conference, led to the Anti-Personnel Landmines Treaty, so too an international conference could put a world spotlight on a principal recommendation from the Final Document of the NPT 2000 Review: "... the total elimination of nuclear weapons is the only absolute guarantee against the use or threat of use of nuclear weapons."[5]

An international conference on nuclear dangers is the original idea of Kofi Annan. He needs a credible state to host it. In holding such a conference, to which all the governments of the world would be invited, including India, Pakistan, and Israel, which do not belong to the NPT, the Government of Canada would contribute greatly to strengthening the role of the UN in nuclear disarmament. Such a concerted effort would advance another important Canadian objective: strengthening the legal regime that underpins the multilateral system. This concentrated attention on the objective of nuclear disarmament – the elimination of nuclear weapons – would re-focus the attention of the public in a truly constructive way. If Sweden can sponsor a new International Commission on Weapons of Mass Destruction, headed by Hans Blix (an action announced in July 2003), why cannot Canada sponsor an international conference to review its findings?

Advancing such a policy may well incur the displeasure, if not the hostility, of the United States. But Pugwash argues:

> It must be explained that the object of the policy is not to counter the U.S., but to advance Canadian interests in breaking out of the incoherent posture we and NATO are now in, and also to save the legal regime for the elimination of nuclear weapons. It is entirely proper for a friendly neighbour to point out to the U.S. that its nuclear weapons policies must implement legal commitments.[6]

Naturally, no one conference can by itself resolve the nuclear weapons crisis. The work of implementing all Thirteen Practical Steps must go on. But the conference would be a method of stimulating renewed international energy. Canadian leadership at this moment would be realistic as well as courageous.

It is the new extreme actions of the United States that render Canada's "balance" approach outdated. Canadians must understand how deeply the terrorist attack of September 11 has affected the American psyche. It has produced a fortress mentality and a new conviction that only the United States can enforce international law and order. The right-wing core of the Bush Administration is using this fear of terrorism to undermine the UN; it wants to render it toothless, to reduce it to a global welfare agency carrying out the orders of the United States. This destruction of the UN's primary role to maintain peace and security in the world will pose the gravest challenge to Canadian foreign policy in the history of Canada–U.S.

relations. The struggle inside Ottawa – about which way to go, with the United States or the UN – will be fierce.

A continued attempt to maintain a "balance" will paralyze Canada's foreign policy over the security issues that are at the core of the UN. To keep the Bush Administration happy, Canada will have to swallow its values. The new Conservative Party will be glad to see this happen and so will the right-wing press. They do not share the values of the UN system as the heart of law and order in the new world. They want more of "Pax Americana." These voices are very loud in Canada and constantly inhibit politicians and government officials who would like to uphold UN values.

The composition of the Cabinet and the assessment of the situation by Canada's prime minister will determine whether Canada will stand up for UN values or cozy up to the United States for the sake of good relations. Lester B. Pearson made his choice for the UN. Brian Mulroney stayed with the United States. Jean Chrétien has tried to be both an internationalist and a continentalist. Now the spotlight falls on Paul Martin. An astute and highly experienced politician, Paul Martin's inclinations may well be to put a foot in both camps. But the Bush Administration will test him early on – to determine if he is "with us or against us."

Martin will inherit a new team of managers installed in the Department of Foreign Affairs and International Trade immediately after the U.S.-Canada fallout from the Iraq war. The instructions they received were to get the relationship back on track. The continentalists argue that Canada simply cannot afford to have the United States mad at it. The internationalists argue that Canada cannot effectively cede its sovereignty to the United States and still remain a country. Who does Canada need more: the United States or the UN? The resolution of that agonizing question will not be done by the managers but by the prime minister himself.

Paul Martin brings to office the internationalist credentials inherited from his father, Paul Martin Sr., one of the great "international" Canadians of the past. He also understands the continentalist argument well and, as a former finance minister, knows where Canada's bread and butter lies. Although Martin was somewhat reluctant to make his policy preferences clear while Chrétien was still prime minister, a speech delivered 30 April 2003 entitled "Canada's Role in a Complex World" does give some clues. In the speech, Martin adopts the cautious approach favoured by Chrétien and characterizes the crisis over Iraq as a failure "of the international community to forge a shared consensus," sidestepping the crucial role of the United States in preventing any consensus from emerging. Other speeches have revealed Martin's support for Canadian participation in the U.S. missile defence program, and his willingness to engage the Canadian military in operations outside of the authorization of the UN Security Council, when such operations are based on Canadian values. However, he has also shown his support of UN initiatives to end the worst forms of poverty and declared a willingness to take account of the opinions of caucus, some of whom oppose Canadian participation in missile defence, when formulating policy. As prime minister, Martin will be forced to more fully expose his position on this essential debate between the continentalist and internationalist approaches.

This will not be just a struggle for Ottawa mandarins, the Liberal caucus, or even the prime minister to sort out. This struggle will be for the soul of Canada. It will play out directly on the steps Canada takes – or does not take – to build the conditions for enduring peace in the world. Kofi Annan believes that the world has entered a "crisis of the international system," and wants this debated by world leaders. In this debate, Canada's vision must go far beyond Canada–U.S. relations and analyze anew world values for peace. Nothing in our past will equal the importance of the looming showdown on values. The public will be deeply involved, and future elections may be fought on the issue. The future foreign policy of Canada will become domestic policy of the highest order.

Notes

1 Press Conference, SG/SM/8803, 30 July 2003.

2 Government of Canada, "Canada in the World: Canadian Foreign Policy Review," 1995.

3 The New Agenda Coalition, founded in 1998, comprises Brazil, Egypt, Ireland, Mexico, New Zealand, South Africa, and Sweden. Its goal is to advance the nuclear disarmament agenda contained in the Non-Proliferation Treaty.

4 Bill Robinson, "Canada and Nuclear Weapons: Canadian Policies Related to, and Connections to, Nuclear Weapons," Project Ploughshares Working Paper 01-5, October 2002.

5 "The Final Document of the 2000 Review Conference of the Parties to the Treaty of the Non-Proliferation of Nuclear Weapons," NPT/CONF.2000/28.

6 Canadian Pugwash Group, "The Only Absolute Guarantee: A Brief on Canada's Nuclear Weapons Policies," presented to DFAIT Foreign Policy Review, April 2003.

CANADIAN MASS MEDIA AND THE MIDDLE EAST

Tareq Y. Ismael and Jacqueline S. Ismael

In a recent study on the Canadian media's portrayal of Muslims and Arabs in Canada and the Middle East following the terrorists attacks in the United States on September 11th, and the subsequent U.S. "war on terrorism," we were amazed by the sheer volume of anti-Arab, anti-Muslim, and anti-dissent materials and opinions contained within mainstream media.[1] Long-standing Canadian commitments to democracy, multiculturalism, tolerance of dissent, and multinational efforts for the maintenance of peace and security seemed to have been abandoned in the emotive response to September 11. However, the bias may be more systemic than that, as coverage of Iraq in the main press reflects similar stereotypes and bias. An example is an article in CanWest Global's *National Post* on 14 April 2003, by Mark Steyn, stating that, as a result of American involvement, "Iraq will be, at bare minimum, the least worst governed state in the Arab world, at best, pleasant, civilized and thriving." Many such core stereotypical images were found in the Canadian press justifying war against Iraq.[2]

It is generally understood that a main function of the news media is to inform the public about current events in the world. The role of informant, however, is not neutral. The media filters information about current events through an ideological matrix. Media bias and self-censorship arise from internalized pre-conceptions, pre-selection of the "right-thinking" people, and the adaptation of reporters and commentators to the realities of ownership constraints based on corporate and political centres of power.[3] This paper explores the nature of the filter that informs the media's coverage of the Middle East.

The Canadian media relies heavily on its American counterparts for acquiring and reporting news, as well as on global newswire services like the British *Reuters*, the French *Agence France-Presse*, and the American *Associated Press* and *United Press International*. These four news agencies account for more than 80 per cent of international news. The two American wire services in particular, while they operate internationally, remain subject to American organizational and political pressures.[4] Thus, foreign news content in the Canadian press is, more often than not, a reproduction of the American news wires and reports from the *New York Times, The Los Angeles Times, Cox News, Knight Rider,* and *Scripps Howard*. Dependence on foreign news content can be attributed to the insignificant presence of the Canadian press in foreign countries. This becomes critical when American foreign reports cover regions in which the American administration has a strong interest, such as the Middle East. In this situation the Canadian consumer receives an almost unadulterated American version of the event depicted as fact and reality.[5] The production of news is never value-free; news does not just happen; ideas and pictures represent reality through an interpretive lens that filters information through a preset paradigm.

The journalist reduces a complex and unmanageable reality into a story or news material according to tacitly agreed upon rules, and in so doing, he or she communicates the core context of the pre-conceptions, prevalent ideas and the implicit assumptions of the larger society, or a particular sector of that society. The core context, here, refers to the paradigm setting, its place in reality, and the implicit values and the attitudes it promotes.[6] Through its reliance on American news services, Canadian coverage of foreign affairs implicitly promotes American foreign policy objectives. For example, in covering the 1982 and 1984 elections in El Salvador, the Canadian media portrayed the elections in essentially the same terms as the American press. In reporting the 1979 Iranian Revolution, the *Globe and Mail*, and the *Toronto Star* depended largely on the American news services and missed the opportunity to report on the Canadian angle of the revolution.[7]

In 2003 the American government strictly controlled the media coverage of the war in Iraq by sponsoring "embedded" journalists to follow the "coalition of the willing" forces. This is evidence of an American policy directly affecting the ability of foreign states, in this case Canadian, to report the war. According to one Canadian reporter, journalists from states that opposed the war were denied access to the war zone. The military command referred to independent journalists as "unilaterals," while "embedded journalists [were] given exclusive access to the war." In an online essay for the CBC, "unilateral" reporter Paul Workman argued that, by "keeping 'unilateral' journalists out of Iraq, the Americans have succeeded in reducing independent reporting of the war, and I believe this was exactly their plan from the beginning."[8] Of course, there is little Canadian news agencies could do to change the policy of the American and British military. Considering that the only journalists with access to the war were "embedded" journalists picked by the Pentagon, the world relied on two sorts of coverage: the "embedded" journalists with access and those reporting on the war from a distance. The CBC reported that there were a thousand reporters, producers, and technicians from around the world who were not allowed into

Northern Kuwait or Iraq to report on the war and were forced to do their work from Kuwait City. This means that Canadian news coverage relied on the official narrative, with limited opportunity or ability to provide alternative interpretations or questions about the war's development. This was seldom mentioned or debated in the Canadian reportage of the war.

Exacerbating this, the Canadian mass media has progressively moved towards concentration in conglomerates. Media barons argue that, as mass media fall into fewer hands, monopoly media markets emerge with more money to invest in quality reportage and more power to withstand pressure from advertisers who might wish to exercise editorial influence. This is contrary to the core arguments in favour of a free press, which maintain that competition breeds choices that are threatened by mergers and acquisitions. A free press is designed to allow for the expression of divergent views about single events or issues, and this helps to ensure that the news media can never be exploited for a private purpose. However, whatever the argument for or against media conglomerates, the fact is that the media are the gatekeepers of information, and what passes through these gates enters into the public consciousness and becomes part of the collective memory. It follows that the more avenues that are open to diverse representations of news, the more media, as an institution, will represent diverse values and dissenting views within a multicultural society.[9] Furthermore, the news media serves as a representation of the truth, meaning that the more these representations are streamlined into one or two acceptable interpretations, the more there is a limitation of the ability for public debate and discourse, two necessary activities for a viable democracy. A centralized and concentrated media has the effect of limiting the public space available for individuals to question what they see in the media, and consequently define for themselves the world around them: the cornerstone of a healthy democracy.

The concentration of Canada's mass media is evidenced in several communication empires. The major players are CanWest Global, Bell Globemedia, Rogers Communications Inc., Quebecor Inc., and Le Groupe Videotron. A focus on the first two illustrates the pitfalls of media concentration. The Asper family owns 45 per cent of CanWest Global. CanWest Global has operations in Canada, Australia, New Zealand, and Ireland. In July 2000, CanWest signed a $3.5-billion deal to purchase a Hollinger-owned controlling interest in the Southam newspaper chain, including all of its newspapers, magazines, and Internet assets. The Hollinger acquisition gave CanWest overlapping television and newspaper coverage in twenty-five out of twenty-six markets, with a 35 per cent share of the Canadian advertising market. The purchase included 15 metropolitan papers and 126 community newspapers. The group covers TV broadcasting that reaches 94 per cent of English-speaking Canada and engages in other related information activities like radio, TV production, advertising, distribution, and multimedia.[10]

Following this CanWest acquisition, professor David Spencer, an expert on newspaper history, said that the deal had serious implications for democratic discourse and added that he was convinced that there was a need for strong counter-voices to behave much like a parliamentary opposition to keep "those folks on their toes, and we just do not have it."[11] In an operating system of free presses, these voices are supposed to be coming from alternate news services and mediums. The late Mr. Asper, former executive chairman of CanWest Global Communications, expressed candidly his opinions on a number of issues in the weekly program *Eye on Media*. Mr. Asper found his critics "blind, one eyed critics"; "CTV has gone out of its way to slag and smash and denigrate Global"; "CBC is dangerous, has become a state within a state and should be expunged"; and the "CRTC must be reformed because license renewal is utterly archaic."[12]

The other media giant is Bell Globemedia, based in Toronto. Bell Canada Enterprises owns 70 per cent, while the Thomson family has the other 30 per cent. Much like CanWest, it encompasses national commercial TV, multimedia, national newspapers, and Internet services. CTV is the largest commercial television network, with wholly owned stations covering 80 per cent of the Canadian market. Bell Globemedia also owns CTV specialty channels that slice out as much as half of the Canadian market, in addition to the *Globe and Mail*, which is the nation's largest newspaper. This media giant employs four thousand people and generates some $4.3-billion revenue, most of it through the Bell Canada arm.[13]

Concerns about homogenization of news were voiced "loud and clear" as a result of the duopoly of the Canadian media system. An October 2001 survey, conducted by the University of British Columbia, on the impact of ownership on content looked specifically at CanWest Global and Bell Globemedia. The results of the survey are indicative, though not conclusive, because the survey compared only the *National Post* (newspaper) and *Global National* (TV channel) from CanWest with the *Globe and Mail* (newspaper) and *CTV News* from Bell Globemedia in a relatively short collection period of only four weeks (between October and November 2001). Nevertheless, the study indicated that there was more cross-promotion and convergence of news among the properties of CanWest Global than among those of Bell Globemedia.[14]

The findings might not be surprising because the factor of proprietorship in CanWest bears significantly on policy, content, and reportage. The late Mr. Asper, by his admission, was a "hands-on" owner. News reporting reflects not only pre-conceived ideas and values but also the implicit assumptions of what is "normal" in the cultural setting of the reportage and the professional communication environment. Mr. Asper, unlike Bell Canada, was vociferous about his views on the culture of the Middle East, the Israeli–Palestinian problem and about his pride in supporting Israeli policies and passionately decrying its critics. News coverage in his papers reflected his views and reinforced his policy of news convergence to get his message across amongst the Canadian public.

The Canadian Radio-television and Telecommunications Commission (CRTC) serves as the national regulator of the telecommunications industry. In July 2003, it called for comments on a list of fifteen proposed new ethnic satellite channels to be offered in Canada before approving the licenses. The application for Al-Jazeera, the Arab news channel based in Qatar and broadcast to North America from Rome, caused the most controversy. The Canadian Jewish Congress, through its president and head of the Quebec region branch, referred to the station as "Osama bin Laden's bullhorn to the world," arguing that it is "virulently anti-Semitic and racist, and likely to contravene Canadian law." Writing in the *Globe and Mail*, John Doyle concludes:

> *It would be best if we could all judge for ourselves. There are laws that govern broadcasting and there are hate laws in Canada. If Al-Jazeera is available here, as it should be, it can be measured against those laws and its carriers in Canada punished if those laws and regulations are broken.*[15]

While Al-Jazeera certainly holds different interpretations of the world, specifically the war in Iraq and the "war on terrorism," this should not be cause for alarm in a multicultural and open society. This hesitation is perhaps a signal that alternative viewpoints have become less acceptable in the mainstream Canadian mass media market. CanWest Global journalist Les MacPherson echoed the calls of the Canadian Jewish

Congress, claiming, "Al-Jazeera is blatantly anti-American and anti-Israel."[16] To take only the "anti-Israel" claim: the Israel–Palestinian conflict is a difficult and emotional issue and is certainly not settled. Large sections of Canada's population remain committed to the idea of Palestinian liberation. Certainly Canada can handle differing interpretations of the current violence in the region. In addition, Al-Jazeera provides an alternative source for world news and representations of the truth that a healthy democracy depends upon.

In sum, the Canadian mass media provides the primary interpretation, not only of the events that take place in the world, but also of issues that are critical to consensus. Mass media operates as a cultural guide to norms and understandings, and it is through these that enemies are defined for the public. Examples of critical matters defined by the mass media are: the right to power, legitimate use of violence, illegitimate opposition to order, and accepted hierarchies among nations. Within Canadian media, references to the war in Iraq have tended to unilaterally defend the American war while discrediting its opposition by labelling those participating in Iraqi resistance as "Saddam loyalists," "terrorists," "Baathists," or those "opposed to freedom," as President Bush likes to say. The wholesale acceptance by Canada's biggest news conglomerates of these loaded terms limits the ability for Canadians to foster alternative and independent viewpoints of the situation in Iraq. The media engineers consensus on the basis of the global media narrative. However, Canadian newspapers are so absorbed into the global narrative that, during the hostage-taking crisis in Beirut in the later 1980s and early 1990s, they paid less attention to the Canadian than to the American and British hostages.[17]

Middle East Reportage
in the Canadian Media

Although Canada has never been an imperial power, nor a colonizing force, it inherited the British legacy of inter-cultural power discourse that is commonly referred to as Orientalism. The fact that Canadian society is premised on multiculturalism does not obviate an ingrained bias that views Canadians as having British values and customs while allowing immigrants to celebrate their past culture on certain occasions, in a formalized manner, after which everyone goes back to the *normal way*, or the British way.

Burdened by the persistence of British ethnocentrism, most Euro-Canadians tend to identify themselves by contrast with non-Euro-Canadians, like the Native people and immigrants that constitute the "other" from the Canadian self. The "other" is an imaginary category that is built from stereotypes that maintain the status quo without factual reference to the actual identity of the imagined "other."[18]

The inter-cultural discourse between a powerful colonizer and a powerless colony underlies the concept of Orientalism, which necessarily emerged and became normal during the era of Imperialism in the nineteenth century. The roots of Orientalism go back centuries, from the epoch of the Crusades and onward. Europeans, in writing about the Middle East and its formative force, Islam, in the thirteenth century, combined wholly inconsistent passages, even extremes of accuracy and inaccuracy for amusement, instruction, and controversy. Even the best-informed minds in that period failed to discriminate between reliable and unreliable sources, combined conflicting material, and sometimes preferred the poorest.[19] The writings on Islam spread the idea that Islam was "a religion of outward forms, the virtuous actions of Muslims were vain, and they could not avail to salvation because in the mediaeval consciousness Islam was not as edifying as Christianity."[20] The Christian medieval canon on Islam survived the Enlightenment and passed to the age of colonization and imperialism to form a congruent and neat underpinning of the power discourse in Orientalism that characterizes the cultures of Europe and North America.

The essential aspects of modern Orientalist theory and practice are premised on an inherited set of past structures that were secularized and reformed by disciplines such as philology, which in turn were modernized and naturalized substitutes for the supernaturalism of medieval Christian understanding. The Christian religious paradigms of human history, encounters with the Muslim east and destiny, were not expunged from Orientalist texts. The religious patterns were simply redeployed and redistributed in a secular framework. First, colonization brought geographic expansion that augmented the biblical frame of reference. Second, there was a historical self-confrontation, which meant that understanding Europe meant also understanding the objective relations between Europe and its previously temporal and cultural frontiers. Third, character-designation, as a physiological-moral classification gathered power. In the nineteenth century it became a genetic type that enhanced moral generalization. In this way, it became possible to refer to the Oriental in his "primitive state," "backward" conditions, or "violent" spirit, and furnished a creative and unflagging source of stereotypes that posited the West in a superior position and sustained that myth into the new millennium.[21]

The popular image fashioned by Orientalism of the "dirty Arab," amply illustrated with the unphotogenic image of Yasser Arafat, competes in the media with the more photogenic image of Saddam Hussein, who personified the uncivilized, unscrupulous, immoral, and sadistic character of "the dirty Arab." In American discourse on both the Palestinian-Israeli conflict and Iraq, these images are used in the place of a serious analysis of the context of violence and conflict. In the lead-up to the American invasion of Iraq, for example, the portrait of Saddam Hussein was overtly used by the White House to obfuscate the unilateralism versus multilateralism debate raging in the Security Council. These images also reverberated in Canadian newspapers. In this Orientalist polemic and imagery, the Arab, the Middle East, and Muslims in general are fixed as transgressors of peace and security in an otherwise civilized world of law and order.[22]

The structure and development of Orientalism took place in the world of European academia and then passed to North America. As such, the concepts and the associated imagery of the "other" versus "us" has pervaded North American culture at various levels through the vehicle of the mass media. The media "raided the cupboard of Orientalism for alimentation, picking up old prejudice and bits of morbid information" in their pursuit of engineering consensus amongst people whose receptive pre-disposition derives from a British cultural legacy of superiority and bias.[23] The media employ stereotypes that derive from structured concepts of Orientalism and continue to define an image of the "other," that sustains a self-image of superiority.

During the expanded "war on terror" and the American-led war in Iraq, similar terms describing the people of the region remained pre-eminent. Specifically, following the declaration of victory by U.S. President George W. Bush, the Canadian media began referring to those resisting U.S. occupation as "suicidal Arabs," "insurgents," "terrorists," "Baathists," and "the kind of savages the allies are fighting." Clearly, the language used is not unbiased. Similarly, although Canada was not a party to war and opposed it diplomatically, Canadian media referred to the U.S.-led military force as the "allies" or "coalition forces" and preferred the term "nation-building" to occupation. Furthermore, the media presented an image of Iraq centred on the image of Saddam Hussein: brutal, corrupt, dictatorial, and inhumane. The images of Saddam's numerous and opulent palaces ran beside pictures of the "looting" Iraqis, and, following the assassinations of Hussein's sons, the media became obsessed with the use of bounties to gain the assistance of local Iraqis. Referring to "post-Saddam Iraq," the media consistently used the terms "de-Baathification," "Iraqization of the new Iraq," and "grinding war of pacification" and adopted the term "hunting" to describe the war's new techniques. While it would be unfair to argue that the Canadian media did not participate in a wider debate about the occupation of Iraq, the debate was centred on how long, or simply how, to occupy the country, avoiding the larger questions of its legality and morality.

Thus we find basic clusters of thematic stereotypes about the Arabs, the Middle East, and Islam that came into more intensive circulation after the rise in oil prices in 1974 and following the Iranian Revolution in 1979. Basic stereotypes are the core reservoir of images that the mainstream media (including their affiliates of "experts" and pundits) use to generate specific rhetoric for a specific event. Stereotyping functions as an ongoing cementing of the legitimization process of the ideological structure and simultaneously justifies a certain policy drawn to deal with any given event. In doing so, the analytical context of the event, as well as different or oppositional views, are usually omitted or slighted. The public is generally left with one resonating dominant discourse from the media.[24] In 1986, the stereotypical cluster of themes that framed mass media references to the Arabs, Islam, and the Middle East – all cognitively linked – were observed to be as follows.[25]

1. The representation of Arab Muslim states in the Middle East as networks of terrorists; and terrorism

as congenital and unrelated to political conflict, or long-standing grievances derived from prior violent intervention;

2. The reduction of Islamic discourse to extremist fundamentalist doctrines advocating political violence and repression of human rights;

3. The dissociation of outbreaks of violence in the Middle East from their historical and political context, associating these with ethnic and religious diversity;

4. The association of civilization and democracy in the Middle East with Israel, while neglecting its systematic violation of human rights, Security Council resolutions, and international law;

5. The equation of Arab opposition to Israel with anti-Semitism.

Combinations and permutations of these themes constructed the mainstream media portrayal of events in the Middle East, adding in time more evocative images to the imaginings of Orientalism. In addition to the 'fabulously wealthy barbaric Arab,' there emerged the 'sex maniac with penchant for white slavery' and the 'naturally predisposed terrorists.' The media employ such evocative phrases to build the frame of reference in which the Western audiences internalize the essence of the Arabs and their culture. The intermingling of the stereotypes generates the understanding that violence in the region is linked to the nature of Islam and its adherents; this image in turn dovetails into the Arabs as indolent, oversexed, and brutish sheiks who misused their oil wealth in the pursuit of worldly pleasures and/or fanatical power. This exposition of the Arabs is frequently juxtaposed against the technological, cultural, and intellectual superiority of the West.[26]

A kaleidoscope of the same stereotypical themes has been in place for more than two decades. However, after the tragedy of

September 11 when the American media's rallying cry (which the Canadian media echoed) became one of war on terrorism and terrorists, these stereotypes were overtly legitimized by those with power and authority to set public discourse. While the U.S. or Canadian media are not monolithic, dissenting views from the main Orientalist discourse are few and usually buried in the avalanche of consensus-manufacturing articles and op-eds. For example, right after September 11, Eric Margolis, an internationally syndicated columnist who writes in the *Toronto Sun*, was invited by "Bynon" on cable channel 49 (Prime Time) to talk on the event. Based on his knowledge of Afghanistan, he maintained that neither the resources of Osama bin Laden nor the tribal mentality of the Taliban could have orchestrated such a sophisticated act. He was not invited back.

In the wake of 9/11, the mainstream media accepted the U.S. government's version at face value and voluntarily censored any critical investigation of the event. Such absence of scrutiny underlines the impact of the media propaganda in filtering information to the public and blocking the process of public scrutiny. In contrast, in Europe there has been more than one attempt to raise penetrating questions about the validity and authenticity of the evidence presented by the U.S. government.[27] The contrast became manifest in the Security Council debates over the passage of a resolution to sanction the U.S. invasion of Iraq. Contrary to its usual alignment with the United States on Middle East policy, and to the chagrin of the United States, Canada was an active participant in the debate. The Canadian public broadcasting service (CBC), both radio and television, provided a forum for the public airing of all stakeholders in the debate to enlighten the Canadian public fully on the issues involved and their multifaceted implications. However, this kind of scrutiny has not carried over to the post-invasion situation in Iraq. Like Afghanistan, events in Iraq are detached from their context and from policy. To illustrate my point, we quote from a recent email sent by a colleague:

> *I talked this morning to my sister [in Baghdad] for about a half hour. She told me stories you cannot believe. She wept and was so demoralized. Being a doctor and a humanist, she felt that she would never see such a thing done by any occupier. American troops going to houses, throwing people out, pillaging, stealing, and shooting if they feel like it! Abu Dhabi, Al-Jazeera, and other TV and radio stations reported on these. She said even their reports are very unusual as they state it in the most blatant terms.*

There has been a virtual blackout in North America of any critical news stories coming out of Iraq. The core context for the war remains, unquestioned and unscathed: that the U.S.-led war in Iraq is a war of liberation and a democratic mission to bring peace and freedom to a troubled region. Through design or circumstance, the Canadian news media have forgone their responsibility to Canadians to be a critical, responsible, and independent window to the world.

Notes

1 Tareq Y. Ismael and John Measor. "Racism and the North American Media Following September 11: The Canadian Setting," *Arab Studies Quarterly* (spring 2003).

2 E.g., *Toronto Star*, 16 April 2003; *National Post*, 4 October 2002; *National Post*, 1 April 2002; *Globe and Mail*, 18 March 2003.

3 Edward S Herman and Noam Chomsky, *Manufacturing Consent: the Political Economy of Mass Media* (New York: Pantheon Books, 2002), ix, 1.

4 Ibid., 335.

5 Karim H. Karim, *Islamic Peril, Media and Global Violence* (Montreal: Black Rose Books, 2000), 14.

6   Edward Said, *Covering Islam* (New York: Vintage Books, 1997), 47–50.

7   Karim, *Islamic Peril, Media and Global Violence*, 14–15.

8   Paul Workman, "Embedded journalists versus 'unilateral' reporters," 7 April 2003. http://www.cbc.ca/news/iraq/canada/correspondents_workman030407.html

9   Erin Willis, "Concentration of Ownership in the Mass Media: A Threat to the Free Exchange of Information?" 18 August 1995, *Critical Mass* Issue 3; http://www.peak.sfu.ca/cmass/issue3/concentration.html

10 Calson Analytics Media Resource, "ketupa.net media profiles: Asper &CanWest Global," April 2003. http://www.ketupa.net/asper.htm.

11 Communications and Public Affairs, University of Western Ontario, 31 July 2000. http://comms.uwo.ca/media/archives/commentary/2000/may_aug/july31.htm

12 iChannel TV. http://www.ichanneltv.com/programs/promos/asper_release.html

13 Calson Analytics Media Resource, "ketupa.net media profiles: Asper &CanWest Global," April 2003. http://www.ketupa.net/bce.htm.

14 Liam Mitchell et al., "Homogenizing news or maximizing resources?" December 2001. http://www.journalism.ubc.ca/thunderbird/2001-02/december/ownership.html

15 John Doyle, "Maybe it's time we saw Al-Jazeera for ourselves," *The Globe and Mail* (16 July 2003), R2.

16 Les MacPherson, "Why do we need Al-Jazeera when we have the CBC?", *Saskatoon Star-Phoenix* (17 July 2003), A3.

17 Karim, *Islamic Peril, Media and Global Violence*, 15.

18 James Crawford, http://www.usask.ca/education/coursework/802/papers

19 Norman Daniel, *Islam and the West: the Making of an Image* (Oxford: One World, 1993), 261.

20 Ibid., 253.

21 Edward Said, *Orientalism* (New York: Vintage Books, 1979), 119–22.

22 Ibid., 285–87.

23 Karim, *Islamic Peril, Media and Global Violence*, 59.

24 Said, *Covering Islam*, ix–xviii.

25 Karim, *Islamic Peril, Media and Global Violence*, 61–62.

26 Ibid., 62–63.

27 Thiery Meyssan, *9-11: The Big Lie* (London: Carnot Publishing, 2002). See also http://www.asile.org/citoyens/numero13/ pentagone/erreurs_en.htm

THE JOHN WAYNE FALLACY: HOW LOGIC CAN HELP US LOSE OUR FAITH IN VIOLENCE

Trudy Govier

Among the many factors that contribute to our acceptance of war and violence is bad logic. This claim may seem surprising, in the light of other notorious causes of political violence such as greed, competition for power and domination, racism, social inequality, and imperialism. Feelings of fear, humiliation, resentment, and revenge are also powerful factors; so too are religious differences and value disagreements about justice, democracy, and freedom. Many factors influence our acceptance of the recourse to physical violence, but in all this, our reasoning matters too. It plays a central role in the arguments we use to justify policies and actions. There is an abundance of careless argument and faulty logic in our reflections about physical violence. Not only do leaders and pundits use and repeat bad arguments when seeking to justify violence to the public, members of the public often swallow the discourse uncritically, reproducing the fallacies with fatal effect.

The John Wayne Fallacy[1]

A major problem with our thinking about violence is the highly unrealistic nature of expectations about what it can accomplish. Among the many sources of this error is the fact that our expectations come more from dramatic narratives than from life itself. Think, for instance, of western movies. Plots are structured around a competition between the Good Guys and the Bad Guys. As these stories are told, the Bad Guys, who are truly and fully bad (no ambiguities here), have caused some sort of problem that has to be solved. A quick and efficient solution is needed. The Good Guys will have to win a victory over the Bad Guys in a violent struggle, after which they will eliminate the Bad Guys, preferably by killing them off. The physical violence of the struggle makes for drama and excitement, and the victory of the Good Guys provides a satisfying and tidy end to the story. In a typical final scene, the Good Guy, in the person of John Wayne or some similarly masculine type, stands victorious holding his rifle at his side. Or he strides triumphantly off into an orange and pink sunset – the implication being that he is leaving a much better world behind him.

It's a stark struggle between Good and Bad and the moral of the story is clear: the Good are entitled to use physical violence against the Bad and they can win a moral victory, and solve a serious Problem when they do. That's conflict at the movies.

The basic dichotomy between good and bad or good and evil needs to be questioned – and we'll come to that point later. But first let's scrutinize the tidy ending. The narrative ends at the point of victory, when the conquering hero has supposedly made his world happy and safe. But in real life – as distinct from the movies – there are serious after-effects when physical violence is used.[2] War, terrorism, and violent revolution are notoriously painful in appalling ways. People are killed and injured, usually in strikingly large numbers, and many suffer terribly. The resentment and hatred in survivors propels quests for retaliation and revenge; thus violence has a decided tendency to provoke more of itself. Needed facilities for water, sewage, medical treatment, schools, and power generation are disrupted, with the result that millions of vulnerable people lack necessities of modern life. Physical and cultural environments are seriously damaged. Economies are shattered. The people who live through all this are real human beings, not characters on a screen.

John Wayne and the other heroes of violent drama never have to clean up after the struggle. Movies never show the great masculine heroes removing debris, treating the sick and injured, rebuilding hospitals, schools, highways, and bridges, or restoring power lines and factories – much less facing tasks of reconciliation so that coexistence becomes possible. Dramatic narratives have form, form that is lacking in life itself. People write narratives and among their narratives are these standard scripts, which move to a tidy ending and omit the mess of reconstruction. In the real world, violent struggles do not end neatly. The aftermath of violence is nearly always a situation in which injured, frightened, starving, and furious people try to cope with dislocation and hunger while warding off attacks from the victorious.

Forgetting about the aftermath might be all right if you're writing scripts, but it's desperately misleading if you're thinking how to resolve a serious political conflict. The John Wayne fallacy occurs when we assume life will be like the movies and infer that once the militarily victorious party has triumphed, there will be no further problems. The faulty comparison and its implication that the aftermath is nothing make violence look good. Media coverage of conflicts tends to contribute to the John Wayne fallacy, because when the drama and excitement of the physical adventure end, coverage stops.[3] Rarely if ever do we read reports about grieving relatives, struggling doctors and teachers, UN peacekeepers trying to monitor wobbly borders, shaky ceasefires, and devastated hospitals. Just a little common sense should tell us that killing and generalized, authorized mayhem will produce an awful mess in physical and human terms. But there is little to encourage us to reflect on such facts and much to distract us. So we don't reflect. It's a big mistake.

False Dichotomies

False dichotomies are another aspect of stereotypical narratives of conflict. A dichotomy, of course, is a binary opposition; a false dichotomy is what you get when you treat such an opposition as purely and simply binary, even though it's not.[4] To see this, think of some binary contrasts: good/evil; friend/enemy; beautiful/ugly; fat/thin. In dichotomous thinking, what is good is not bad and what is bad is not good. He who is friend is not enemy, and he who is enemy is not friend. It all seems trite, but reasonable. Call these oppositions *contraries*.[5] We couldn't get along without contraries because distinctions are essential for language and logic. But contraries can be problematic in some deep ways, because we so easily turn them into contradictories. We begin to think of the binary oppositions as exhaustive, when they are not. Take "beautiful" and "ugly," for example. Obviously, many people and many things are neither beautiful nor ugly, but something in between. The same can be said of "fat" and "thin" and – to more closely approach the situation of conflict – "friend" and "enemy." Your friend is not your enemy and your enemy is not your friend – but many people are neither friend nor enemy. To believe otherwise is to engage in paranoiac thinking and step along a route to insanity. For all these contrary predicates, there is an important middle range of indeterminacies, borderline cases, and ambiguities.

We too easily distort spectrum concepts so as to omit that middle range. We use our concepts to mark the extreme ends of the spectrum and neglect to consider the substantial middle. President George W. Bush's statement, shortly after the attacks of September 11th, that "you are either with us or with the terrorists" is a classic example of a false dichotomy. It was a rhetorical attempt to structure the world into Good and Evil, leaving honest intellectuals and skeptics no place to stand.

The idea that the Bad Guys are worse than Bad, being, in fact, Evil, and even members of an Axis of Evil, supports an especially insidious polarization. The term "evil" is so strong that we are highly unlikely to accept that it has any application to our own side. ("I might have a fault or two, I might have done some bad things on occasion, I might have a few flaws of character, sure; but I would never actually be *evil* – and the same is true for my group and my nation. Mistakes maybe, sins occasionally, but evil? Never.") The rhetoric of the Bush administration implies a dangerously distorted picture of a world polarized between good and evil. Not only do the theological overtones of the flawed logic suggest a need for a Crusade or Holy War, the emotional overtones of the word "evil" are strong enough to create enemies by themselves. In fact, the defence analyst Gwynne Dyer explained North Korea's nuclear threats in just this way, interpreting them as a result of that country's shocked anger at suddenly being made a member of an "axis of evil."[6] Stark and exaggerated dichotomies of good and evil, friend and enemy, can polarize reality as well as thought. When we think in false dichotomies of *either/ors*, we over-simplify and fail to consider the *neither/nors* – instances of ambiguity, complexity, indeterminacy that for various reasons fall in the middle of spectrum we have severed into two poles.

False dichotomies don't always concern our classifications of people and things. There are plenty of false dichotomies regarding action and policy. In this context, false dichotomies take the form of failing to consider alternatives. People, including even many well-educated policy analysts, are so ready to assume we face the stark choice between responding with violence and doing nothing at all. "Well what *are* you going to do? Just sit there?" people will ask, expecting and hoping that the critics of violence can provide no answer. They assume that if we reject violence, we will do nothing at all.

But the argument based on omitting alternatives is a kind of manipulation. Alternatives do exist. It's not true that we had a choice between authorizing war on Iraq and doing nothing. That false dichotomy neglects such alternatives as the prolonged and intrusive presence of international inspectors in Iraq or the exiling of Saddam Hussein from his country. The same can be said of the manipulative warning in February 2003 that members of the UN Security Council faced a stark choice between supporting the U.S. position on Iraq and making the United Nations irrelevant to issues of international security. In this case, the false dichotomy structured a threat.

Our Side Bias

The situation of the United Nations points to another subject: unilateralism on the part of the United States.[7] This, you might say, is far from a matter of reasoning. Doesn't such unilateralism find its sources in power? More specifically, the unparalleled military, economic, and cultural power that make the United States the world's only remaining superpower? And the culture and history of the United States, which contribute to its quite particular sense of its historical uniqueness and special destiny? You could ask what reasoning and logic have to do with all this. I think that question can be answered because making an exception of your own case is a form of *inconsistency* or *bias* in favour of your own side. Unilateralism, which is tremendously tempting, especially for the powerful, is a pronounced expression of a partisan bias. We can call it *"our side bias."*

So far as war and violence are concerned, the temptations of *our side bias* arise from the fact that the devastation wrought by violence is obvious and severe when *we* experience it on *our side*, but less obvious and (apparently) not severe at all when *we* impose it on *them*. The three thousand deaths from the terrorist attacks on the United States on September 11th, were deplorable, awful, and painful – and were understood and publicized as such. The destruction was costly and horrendous, and we heard about that. But killings by American and other forces in Iraq, Kosovo, Afghanistan, and elsewhere receive relatively little attention in most western media. We feel pain in our own bodies, not in others; we live our lives in our own countries, not those others; our media cover our interests, and not those others. To sit in a bomber is one thing; to sit under a bomb, another. Thus, *our side bias* is likely to seem natural to many people.

In October, 2001, Tony Blair travelled through the Middle East in an effort to persuade a number of Middle Eastern leaders of the justifiability of bombing Afghanistan as an element of the "war against terrorism." Blair was surprised to find that many leaders did not follow his reasonings on the topic of justifying violent responses to conflicts. They didn't classify suicide bombers as terrorists; in fact, they didn't even think these attackers were committing suicide. They were martyrs and heroes. Blair, who failed to understand that double standard, seemed to feel no doubt about preaching according to a double standard of his own. To him, bombing by a state, even with resultant deaths of innocent civilians, would clearly be properly authorized and legitimate, whereas, in contrast, explosive attacks by non-state agents killing innocent civilians were clearly deplorable and merited the terminal epithet, "terrorism." Thus, double standards abound. In this context, Blair's was a bias in favour of states and against non-state agents.

The case of weapons of mass destruction in Iraq provides an even more powerful example of *our side bias*. Assume, as is plausible, that it is dangerous and seriously wrong for a nation to use weapons of mass destruction. Assume, as is also plausible, that any nation could at some point have leaders who could make risky and unwise decisions. The conclusion would seem to mandate generalized disarmament: it is dangerous for *any* nation to possess weapons of mass destruction. In the fall of 2002 and the winter of 2003, there was an enormous amount of discussion about weapons of mass destruction in Iraq – whether there were any, whether they were hidden, whether and how they had been destroyed, whether inspectors were finding any. Long speeches were given; maps and drawings were provided; satellite pictures were analyzed; Britain's MI5 plagiarized a graduate student paper and Colin Powell, in turn, copied from them; inspectors submitted huge reports; Iraq submitted a twelve-thousand-page document about the state of its weapons.

No such weapons have been located. There was intense criticism on the point, both in the United States and in the United Kingdom. Queries were raised about the quality of the intelligence reports and the reliability of those, inside and outside government, who had expressed their firm conviction such weapons existed in large numbers, were a threat to the world, and legitimated the attack on Iraq. The situation seems to have involved a mix of sloppy evidence-gathering and reasoning, absence of critical thinking, self-deception, and deception and manipulation of others.

In the context of *our side bias*, what is noteworthy here is that virtually *nothing* was said about the possession of weapons of mass destruction by the United States, Britain, France, and other nuclear powers. The whole debate illustrated a double standard between the West and the Others; this was pernicious selectivity, an especially clear case of *our side bias*. Any human beings, anywhere, could be killed or maimed by weapons of mass destruction: biological, chemical, or nuclear. Human life on earth could be terminated by nuclear weapons. Any human being has a warrant to be worried and a right to protest these weapons; it's a universal. The second dimension of universality is that these weapons are threatening and dangerous in any hands and in any country. The United States could have a rash leadership ready to act prematurely and place the peoples of this earth in great danger, in order to pursue what it understands as its own interests. Weapons of mass destruction are an appalling threat in the hands of Saddam Hussein and in the hands of George W. Bush or any other leader. It is an enormous and multi-faceted problem – not, incidentally, a problem likely to be overcome by killing the Bad Guys. And it is a general problem, not a problem restricted to Iraq and North Korea and some other "evil" regimes. To think that only *their* weapons of mass destruction are problematical, while *ours* are necessary and safe amounts to an egregious form of *our side bias*.

False Analogies

To list all the errors of reasoning connected with our thinking about violence is not possible here, but one more form of reasoning deserves special attention: arguing by analogy. In principle, this approach should have something to offer because the teachings of history could hardly be applied in any other way. In practice, though, arguments from historical analogy are often shockingly weak. The all-time favourite strategy is to enlist the assistance of Hitler, who is compared to a contemporary demonized leader. Because war was needed to defeat Hitler, it's claimed that, in virtue of the analogy, we also need war in the current case. Pretty well everybody agrees about Hitler and the need for a war against him, so critics of contemporary militarism can be made to look very naïve and very bad when they are portrayed as defenders of the "appeasement" of 1939. A moment's thought should suffice to show that this is propaganda, not serious analysis.

But more recent analogies are problematic too. All too often, a complex situation of the past is summed up in a kind of "nutshell" description, telling us what lesson *history* supposedly *taught* in that case.[8] Then, on the cavalier assumption that the present situation resembles this past one, the supposed lesson is applied to the present. In the case of Iraq, it is often argued, based on the bombings of Serbia/Kosovo by NATO forces in 1999 and Afghanistan by the United States and Britain in 2001, that bombing from a height can defeat a regime and bring something better, with few or no deaths to "our side." Supposedly, these military campaigns were successful; thus – or so the reasoning goes – the same kind of success may be anticipated in Iraq. These precedents were cited as supporting the claim that bombing Iraq might be a good way to establish a better regime in that country and the even more ambitious claim that such a regime change could begin the building of a more democratic Middle East. The analogies are weak here, and the arguments entirely implausible.

First of all, both in the case of Serbia/Kosovo and in the case of Afghanistan, the nutshell summary of "success" is just plain incorrect, The situation for human rights in Kosovo after the 1999 war has been deplorable. Over fifty thousand international personnel are involved in running the territory; there are many acrimonious disagreements between Kosovan Albanians and peacekeeping personnel; thousands of revenge attacks have occurred; and Serb and gypsy women require the escort of international peacekeepers to do their grocery shopping in safety. The question of whether Kosovo will gain independence from Serbia and Montenegro is still unresolved. More than four years after the "success" of this campaign, the Canadian Department of Foreign Affairs and International Trade warns that the area is too dangerous to be a suitable destination for Canadian travellers. In Serbia, Milosevic, a nationalist and undemocratic leader who had sponsored ethnic cleansing in Bosnia and Kosovo, was defeated in *election polls* on the basis of a *non-violent* electoral campaign. He was not defeated as a direct result of NATO bombing.[9] As for Afghanistan, some two years after the defeat of the Taliban regime and the much-advertised establishment of law and democracy in that country, there is little rule of law. Warlordism, corruption, and chaos prevail, and in some village areas, families who send their daughters to school are threatened with punishment by death. In the meantime, funds for reconstruction, promised by many countries after the defeat of the Taliban, have not been provided by the international community. Taliban and al-Qaeda forces are regrouping in some areas to stage guerrilla attacks and the Karzi government survives only with considerable protection from international forces. Due to opposition by the United States, there are no peacekeeping personnel outside the Kabul area. As with Kosovo, it's a gross understatement to say that bombing "succeeded" in bringing a better order to Afghanistan.

The nutshell premises on which analogy arguments from Kosovo and Afghanistan are erected are simply false. Far from being a sensible application of sensitive historical analysis to contemporary problems, such arguments amount to careless coffee shop analysis at best and manipulative propaganda at worst. And clearly, the similarities between Iraq and these other places is superficial in any event. Even if it were true that bombing had "worked" against Serbia and then Afghanistan under the Taliban regime, those cases wouldn't support a prediction that it would "work" against the solidly entrenched and resource-rich regime of Saddam Hussein.

The Overall "Justification" of Violence

In their most general form, arguments to justify violence have a common structure, one that is quite simple. First, there is a just or morally defensible goal that we must reach by some means or other. Second, by using physical violence as a means, we can arrive at that goal. Third, no other means will get us there. From these premises, we arrive at the conclusion that physical violence is justified "as a last resort." Now there is nothing fallacious in principle about arguments of this general type. They need not involve any erroneous *reasoning* in moving from the premises to the conclusion. Rather, the problem with such arguments is that we are far too ready to accept the premises.

Our side bias tends to make us indulgent in judging our own goals. Often, motives are mixed and goals are confused. In the case of Iraq, President George W. Bush shifted from a rhetoric of "weapons of mass destruction," to "regime change," to "Iraq helped al-Qaeda and other terrorists and has to be stopped," to "We're beginning to build a more democratic Middle East." In the meantime, his critics and even some of his supporters were convinced that access to oil and ensuring his own re-election were major motivations. Prime Minister Tony Blair shifted his public rhetoric from "security against attack by this evil tyrant" to "moral need for protection for human rights in Iraq." If violence is going to be justified as a *means* of reaching a morally respectable *goal*, we have to know what that goal is. We also have to know that it is morally defensible. These conditions were simply not met in the case of the Iraq war. That's the first problem with the general argument for attacking Iraq.

The second problem comes with the premise that physical violence will actually "work" in the sense that it will get us to the goal we seek. It often doesn't, and we too often dismiss that fact because we ignore what happens in the aftermath. (This is where John Wayne comes in.)[10]

Now, we arrive at the third premise, to the effect that there is no alternative means towards our goal except that of physical violence. It's rarely true if it ever is: this sort of premise gets much of its superficial plausibility from the false dichotomy of doing something violent or doing nothing at all.

I'm convinced that better logic would make us more cautious about the use of violence in response to political conflict. A little skepticism could save a lot of lives. Fallacies and careless reasoning are not unique to the topic of violence, but in contexts of war, terrorism, and other forms of political violence, professed justifications deserve our most rigorous attention. Because the destruction and suffering they legitimate are so horrendous, they must be scrutinized carefully: lives are at stake.

Notes

1   I have invented this name; though the mistake is common, this is not a fallacy of the textbooks.
2   There are, of course, movies that are "western" in the sense of dealing with early western U.S. history and its conflicts but are more subtle and nuanced. What I have in mind here is the standard script.

3   The Iraq war of 2003 may turn out to be an exception in this regard. If so, we can only hope that salutary lessons will be learned from the coverage.

4   A dichotomy may be false for different reasons. The alternatives presented may not be exclusive; they may not be exhaustive; they may be neither exclusive nor exhaustive. Furthermore, these conditions may exist for different reasons. I suspect that some of the logical distinctions between such cases (ambiguity, failure of a category to apply at all, category applying in some respects but not others, ill-founded category, for instance) may be of interest in conflict situations. However, the matter cannot be pursued here.

5   This distinction is explained in Chapter Seven of the fifth edition of my text, *A Practical Study of Argument* (Belmont, CA: Wadsworth 2001).

6   Gwynne Dyer, lecture, 5 March 2003, University of Calgary. Relying on reports from David Frum, the Canadian speechwriter who was the original author of the "axis of evil" phrase, Dyer claimed that North Korea was included almost arbitrarily. It was assumed that anything that counts as an "axis" needs more than two members and it would be impolitic to have only Muslim countries on the "axis." According to Dyer, North Korea reacted with shock and horror to being included, and the political struggles between it and the United States were greatly aggravated by the polarized rhetoric of evil.

7   As noted (and decried) by many commentators, including some prominent ones within the United States, this unilateralism has nuances, and subtleties and understand that no situation can provide an uncontroversial recipe for handling another. This is not to say that history should be irrelevant to policy, only that the specious analogies that are so often exploited in public debate are highly unreliable guides to policy.

9   For a brief discussion of what caused the fall of Milosevic, see Gene Sharp, "Serbia's Struggle for Freedom," *Peace Magazine* (October–December 2001): 81–20. I discussed this account in my essay, "Power," in *A Delicate Balance: What Philosophy Can Tell Us about Terrorism* (Boulder, CO: Westview, 2002).

10 This essay was first written in February 2003 and revised in the spring and summer of that year. During this period it became increasingly clear, and was admitted even by insiders in the United

States, that planning with regard to "the peace" and the need to reconstruct after the violence of war had been grossly inadequate. It became glaringly obvious that winning a short-term military victory was far easier than rebuilding an ordered working society in the aftermath.

THE HUMANITARIAN DIMENSION
OF U.S.-IRAQ RELATIONS

Colleen Beaumier, M.P., and Joyce Patel, M.A.

In prosecuting the war on Iraq, the United States and its allies
have failed to garner a significant degree of legitimacy from
the international community. Various Western governments,
legal scholars, and citizens of the world have opposed the war,
challenging the thesis that a military invasion both satisfies
standards of international law and serves the interests of
the Iraqi people. Debate over justification for the invasion
continues. However, this debate will not be explored at
great length in this paper. Rather, this paper addresses the
humanitarian consequences of U.S.–Iraqi relations. In doing
so, the analysis proceeds by placing the humanitarian crisis in
Iraq within a historical context, highlighting the cumulative
effect of U.S. policies toward Iraq. The paper argues that the
U.S. invasion and occupation is but one stage in the overall
process that has led to a humanitarian crisis. The humanitarian
crisis that has visited Iraq for many years and the subsequent
toll the invasion has taken on its population should not be
understood as a single policy or imperative but must be seen as
a continuation of strategies coloured by a doleful lack of vision
and an abiding neglect for the Iraqi people.

It is important to note that the Iraqi situation did not simply result from the actions of a single government. While this
may be true, and many governments played a role in shaping

the humanitarian nightmare in Iraq, this paper will focus on U.S. policy. The focus is neither arbitrary nor representative of an overt bias against U.S. foreign policy. Instead, the emphasis on the United States demonstrates that the current crisis in Iraq is not simply the product of an evil dictator. Rather, the current situation is another stage in the development of U.S.–Iraqi relations.

Moreover, because the Bush administration represents the central proponent of a military invasion, it is instructive to examine the current policy within a historical context. The purpose is to show that the United States has rarely been driven by a concern for humanitarian issues and does not seem to be deviating significantly – notwithstanding the rhetoric coming from the Bush administration – from this characterization with its current invasion of Iraq.

Genocide Sanctioned: U.S.–Iraq Relations before the Gulf War

In the 1980s, the United States and Iraq were allies in a war against the radical Islamic government in Iran. Saddam Hussein exhibited the same brutal tendencies then but was considered manageable by the United States. In fact, President Reagan sent then special envoy Donald Rumsfeld to Baghdad to solidify the alliance and testify to Saddam Hussein's "moderation" relative to the Iranian regime.

The U.S. administration knew Saddam Hussein possessed chemical weapons and that he used these weapons against Iran and later against his own Kurdish populations. Despite the fact that Iraq contravened international law and was arguably responsible for genocide in Halabja, it continued to receive support from the United States in the form of "dual-use" equipment such as helicopters and chemicals. Most notably, the Reagan administration, while publicly denouncing these actions, nevertheless blocked the *Prevention of Genocide Act* and failed to punish Iraq substantively for its violations of the *Geneva Protocol on Chemical Weapons*, to which Iraq was a signatory.

In calling for regime change, the Bush administration used the accusation of Saddam Hussein having gassed his own people. This is true. Hussein's regime did attack the Kurdish villages in northern Iraq in 1987–88. However, what is unclear is the responsibility that the United States bears by virtue of its continued support for the Iraqi regime (part of the U.S. support for Iraq in the Iran-Iraq War). The fact that the United States provided Iraq with billions in loans and agricultural and export credits during the 1980s is a matter of public record. What is striking is its continued support even after the Kurdish massacre. The public condemnation of Iraq by the United States, following Halabja, was followed, paradoxically, with an increase of U.S. economic support that continued to bolster Iraq's weapons program. Humanitarian issues, clearly, did not occupy a central concern for the Reagan administration.

The pertinent question remains: why did the United States support Saddam after he committed these atrocities? It seems clear that during the 1980s Saddam Hussein's regime served salient U.S. economic and military interests in the region. Iraq was engaged in a war against the radical Islamic government of Ayatollah Khomeini in Iran. The United States feared an Iranian victory that could lead to the spread of radical Islam jeopardizing the strategically important and oil-rich Gulf states. In addition, severing economic ties with Iraq was seen as economically detrimental to American business interests and ultimately not a politically prudent objective for the Reagan administration. Rather than overtly inditing the Reagan administration as directly responsible for the genocide against the Kurds, a more circumspect analysis argues that the United States played a tacit role in sanctioning the actions of Hussein's regime by not explicitly punishing his use of chemical weapons. This tacit support of Hussein's actions amounted to a real and present humanitarian crisis in the form of genocide.

Several lessons can be drawn from these incidents that have a direct bearing on humanitarian concerns. First, despite a tangible humanitarian crisis in the form of genocide, the United States did not intervene because this would undermined its own self-interests, and, secondly, since it allowed Iraq to commit massive atrocities, Hussein possibly calculated that any incursion into Kuwait would be met with similar inaction on the part of the United States. What Saddam Hussein did not realize is that an invasion of Kuwait would not be countenanced because it directly affected U.S. interests in the region.

The Gulf War and the Era of Sanctions

Iraq's invasion of Kuwait was met with a UN-countenanced military campaign in January 1991. The immediate impact of the Gulf War was some fifty to one hundred and twenty thousand military deaths and four to fifteen thousand civilian deaths. In addition to deaths, injuries, and displacements, Iraq's economy, infrastructure, health system, and environment were adversely impacted. The Gulf War was a humanitarian disaster for the Iraqi people, who endured intense bombing and then had to survive in a depleted economy. Further, the war caused the collapse of Iraq's once-independent civilian economy. The imports-dependent industrial base was severely affected as imports rapidly became unavailable. The destruction of Iraq's oil industry resulted in a fall in GDP, and this in turn led to a decrease in investment and reconstruction. After ten years of sanctions, over 70 per cent of civilian industrial enterprise became obsolete or operated at a much-reduced level. A once-large and well-trained technical and professional class was reduced to dependence on the state. With 60 to 75 per cent of the workforce unemployed and inflation rates rampant, the Iraqi population became dependent on handouts for survival.

The social effects of this devastation included the development of an underground economy, increases in smuggling and the sex trade, as well as child labour and begging. Like children, women suffer in a unique way as a result of military conflict. Before the 1990s, Iraq was a leader in the Arab world in promoting education and employment for women. The Gulf war resulted in widowhood, rising unemployment, and a widening educational gap that adversely affected the status of Iraqi women, in particular rural women. An important indicator of socio-economic health is a country's infant mortality rate. Immediately before the Gulf War, infant mortality in Iraq fell to 65 per thousand live births, better than the average in the developing world at 76. By 1998 that number rose to 103, with an under-five mortality rate similar to Haiti, Uganda, Senegal, and Yemen. By 2000, the UN Human Development Index ranked Iraq's development level 126th out of 174. A study conducted by Harvard University estimates child and infant mortality increased more than threefold in 1991. These indicators are striking, given that Iraq had been a fairly urbanized and technologically developed country.

Before 1991, Iraq was a modern, urbanized society with a developed infrastructure, a steady economy, and good levels of health and education. The Ahtisaari UN report suggests that, after the Gulf War, Iraq was relegated to a pre-industrial era. Iraqi infrastructure (already significantly damaged as a result of an eight-year conflict with Iran) was further decimated after 1991. Although the civilian infrastructure was left intact after the Iran-Iraq War (with the exception of the Basra region), the economy was severely weakened. The Gulf War resulted in the destruction of civilian infrastructure and the Iraqi economy. Prior to the Gulf War, one Iraqi dinar was still worth US$3.30. In 2002 one Iraqi dinar was worth one-thousandth of that amount. The devastating toll on infrastructure included the destruction of roads, bridges, and railroads. In addition, water purification systems, sewage treatments, electricity grids, and the oil industry were also destroyed or significantly depleted. Iraq's water and sanitation system was dependent on electricity, which purified and pumped water. As a result of the Gulf War, Iraq's electrical capacity was destroyed. Water treatment plants in large cities such as Baghdad and Basra were destroyed resulting in "a public health crisis" caused by raw sewage dumped in the river system.

The World Health Organization described Iraq's medical facilities and capabilities prior to the Gulf War as first-class. As a result of the war, the Ministry of Health was destroyed and communications and transportation were disabled. Damaged civilian infrastructure (electricity, water, and sanitation systems) led to the re-emergence of infectious diseases such as cholera; typhoid, measles, and diarrhoea. This was exacerbated by a real decline in family income, which contributed to an increase in levels of malnutrition. The devastating impacts on a highly mechanized, electricity-dependent Iraqi society are examined by Eric Hoskins in the book *War and Public Health* (1997). According to Hoskins, the destruction of telecommunications and transport coupled with shortages of medical supplies and equipment led to devastating health consequences for Iraqis. The delivery of essential medicines and primary and preventable health care were interrupted. As health care professionals fled, the effectiveness of the health care system was further diminished.

In addition to the social, economic, and health effects of conventional warfare, the use of chemical and biological weapons during the Gulf War had a lasting environmental impact on Iraq. The massive aerial bombing destroyed chemical and biological factories that dispersed toxins into the environment. This had both respiratory and carcinogenic health effects. Further, landmines and burning oil wells destroyed the environment, killed animals, and contaminated water and soil. The use of depleted uranium and its effects on people and the environment are a matter of some controversy. However, the fact remains that Iraq is facing high levels of cancers and birth defects previously unseen in the region.

Sanctions: The Foundation for an Enduring Humanitarian Crisis

The Gulf War set the groundwork for a sustained sanctions regime that would have a long-term impact on the people of Iraq. In response to its invasion of Kuwait, the United Nations Security Council imposed punitive measures, in the form of comprehensive sanctions, on Iraq. Under these sanctions, all imports into Iraq (except medical supplies) and all exports from Iraq were prohibited. The rationale informing the sanctions regime was premised on the assumption that a sustained policy of restrictive sanctions would ultimately cripple the Iraqi regime. This argument, however, conflicted with the reality of the Iraqi situation. Sanctions did not cripple the regime but in fact enabled Hussein to consolidate his power. The former UN Assistant Secretary-General and humanitarian co-ordinator for Iraq argued that sanctions contributed to the consolidation of the state and reduced the chances for the emergence of an opposition. In political terms, the Iraqi people were not "liberated" by a sanctions regime but instead were hampered from effectively revolting against an oppressive government. Those in favour of the current invasion of Iraq openly recognized that the sanctions regime did not curtail Saddam Hussein's power and have used this fact to launch a more coercive approach in the form of military action. The only empirical consequence of the sanctions that cannot be denied is that the Iraqi people, not the regime, were weakened.

Since 1990, there has been a severe deterioration in the standards of living and degradation of the Iraqi economy with grave consequences for Iraqi society. Chronic malnutrition has affected every fourth child in Iraq under five years of age. The infant mortality rates are among the highest in the world. Only 41 per cent of the population have regular access to clean water and 83 per cent of all schools need substantial repairs. In essence, sanctions must be viewed within this historical context. The sanctions regime was imposed on an already crippled nation. Twelve years of sanctions have contributed to a humanitarian crisis reflected in the death of one million Iraqis, nearly 60 per cent children. It is estimated that some five to six thousand children died every month in Iraq as a result of sanctions.[1]

In 1998, the UN Humanitarian Coordinator and Director of the UN Oil-for-Food Program, Denis Halliday, resigned in protest over the sanctions program. In 2000, Hans von Sponeck, the UN Humanitarian Coordinator who replaced Mr. Halliday also resigned in protest. That same year the head of the UN World Food Program in Iraq, Jutta Burgahrdt, also resigned. Previously, Scott Ritter resigned from the UN weapons inspecting team (UNSCOM) because he argued the United States was utilizing the weapons inspections in order to maintain the sanctions regime and not as a way of disarming Saddam Hussein.

If the sanctions were not effectively limiting Hussein's power, why were they not lifted? There is clearly no easy answer. Even asking the question implies that Western governments refused to recognize the devastation sanctions were causing on the Iraqi people. Simply decrying that the troubles of the Iraqi people are wholly the responsibility of the Hussein regime avoids the role Western governments played in failing to search for alternatives to sanctions. No such objective was pursued, and when the harmful consequences of sanctions became evident, those in favour, like Madeleine Albright, the U.S. ambassador to the UN, callously argued that it was worth it.

The Oil-for-Food Program

After the Gulf War, the international community responded to the humanitarian crisis with Security Council Resolution 986 (1995). The resolution was "a temporary measure to provide for the humanitarian needs of the Iraqi people" through the Oil-for-Food program. The Oil-for-Food program permitted Iraq to sell oil in exchange for "medicine, health supplies, food-stuffs and materials and supplies for essential civilian needs." The amount of oil Iraq was able to extract was subsequently raised, and this translated into resources for humanitarian purposes.

On the surface, it appeared that the negative effects of sanctions were mitigated by the Oil-for-Food program. Food production increased, childhood mortality, which increased after the war and under sanctions, declined, and malnutrition among children under age five, which rose during 1991 to 1996, stabilized. However, the decline in childhood mortality was in the north and was not reflected in figures for south/central Iraq. Further, although malnutrition rates declined, they remained high at 14.6 per cent of children under five. In other words, the Oil-for-Food program was not adequate.

According to a March 1999 report by the UN Office of the Oil-for-Food program, since the 1991 Gulf War, Iraq dropped from "relative affluence to massive poverty." The Oil-for-Food program was initially intended to provide humanitarian relief in the form of food and medicine. The World Health Organization, the United Nations Food and Agricultural Organization, UNICEF, and the Secretary-General of the UN agreed on the central problem of the Oil-for-Food program – its inability to generate sufficient funds to address the rehabilitation of Iraq's once-modern social and economic infrastructure. The office of the Iraq Oil-for-Food program recognized that the program was "never intended to be a substitute for normal economic activity" but suggested that, as long as Iraq was subjected to comprehensive sanctions, "there is no alternative to the program for addressing the humanitarian situation in Iraq."

Humanitarian Impact of a Military Invasion

The new war in Iraq has resulted in devastating humanitarian consequences for the civilian population as evidenced by the news reports during the war and by the almost daily reports since the war officially ended. Estimates of the dead are in the 3,000–4,000 range with many more wounded and permanently disabled. The post-war lack of security for civilians, the severely damaged infrastructure, the extensive looting, the regular attacks by insurgents on the occupying forces, their supporters and Western agencies like the Red Cross and the UN are all signs of a society in crisis. The ability of Iraqis to cope is not the same as it was in 1991. Prior to the Gulf War, the Iraqi economy was viable, unemployment and poverty levels were lower, and citizens had access to health and education as well as cash and material assets. In short,

Iraqis were in a better socio-economic state to deal with the consequences of the first Gulf War.

Impact on Children

A Canadian medical team was in Baghdad conducting research at the same time that I was visiting Iraq (21–26 January 2003). In a report entitled *Our Common Responsibility: The Impact of a New War on Iraq's Children*, the team, which included ten experts from the Harvard-based International Study Team, predicted a "grave humanitarian disaster" in the case of a new war in Iraq. The report examined the physical and mental state of Iraqi children. Based on data collected in Baghdad, Karbala, and Basra, the findings suggest that Iraqi children have "a great fear" of a new war and that children as young as four and five had clear concepts of the horrors of war.

The study found that half a million Iraqi children suffer from malnourishment: "Iraq's 13 million children are at grave risk of starvation, disease, death and psychological trauma," according to Dr. Samantha Nutt, the team's health expert. In February, the Centre for Economic and Social Rights (CESR) examined the human cost of a new war in Iraq. CESR's prediction that the U.S.-led military operation would trigger the collapse of Iraq's public health, electrical power, and food distribution transportation systems has been confirmed by the reality of the U.S.-British occupation. CESR food security, public health, infrastructure, and medical emergency experts were in Baghdad January 17–30, 2003, conducting research. The CESR report concluded that the Iraqi population is highly vulnerable and will require much greater humanitarian aid in the event of war.

International Humanitarian Law

The laws of war – International Humanitarian Law (IHL) – stipulate that an occupying power or military force that takes control and authority of a region is responsible for the humanitarian needs of the population. According to the Fourth Geneva Convention, an occupying power has an obligation to ensure the supply of food, medicine, hygiene, and public health. All parties to the conflict have a responsibility to "take all necessary precautions to avoid loss of civilian life." The principles of IHL establish the rules of war and have several implications for all parties to a conflict.

First, indiscriminate attacks are prohibited. This includes the use of chemical, biological, radiological, and nuclear weapons as well as cluster bombs and landmines, which are by their nature indiscriminate.[2] IHL prohibits military attacks that have a disproportionate effect on civilians. Therefore, the destruction of water, electrical, or transport infrastructure, which Iraqis depend on for survival, is prohibited. Finally, all parties to the conflict are under an obligation to provide for the free flow of impartial humanitarian assistance. Grave breaches of these laws are considered war crimes.

The Humanitarian and Security Conditions of Refugees

In addition to the socio-economic and environmental costs of a second Gulf War, there are humanitarian consequences for refugees, asylum seekers, and internally displaced Iraqis. A February 2003 report conducted by Human Rights Watch concluded that the war would likely bring "new hardship" to the civilian population and displaced persons creating new refugee outflows. The report has been proven right.

IHL stipulates that civilians are protected from forced displacement.[3] The occupying power must ensure the security of the civilian population and allow civilians to voluntarily move to escape war, both within and outside the state's borders. In the event of conflict, neighbouring states may close their borders for fear of instability within their own countries and the cost of providing for refugees. Under international law, any country in control of "safe havens" must ensure that such camps are secure and that adequate humanitarian assistance is provided to refugees. Under IHL, the occupying power is also responsible for internally displaced persons (IDPs). IDPs are particularly vulnerable. Prior to the invasion there were between 700,000 and one million IDPs in Iraq, the majority of whom were women and children.

Conclusions

This paper identifies three stages of U.S.–Iraqi relations (the period prior to the first Gulf War, the post-Gulf War era, and the U.S.-led invasion of Iraq) and offers positive alternatives to U.S. foreign policy within each historical stage. The occupation of Iraq or what the United States has referred to as post-war planning, including the role of the Iraqi opposition, the UN, and U.S. corporations are not examined. The focus is on the humanitarian dimension of the Iraqi crisis and its historical context. The alternatives presented (adherence and implementation of international law) are guided by a single imperative – the humanitarian consequences of U.S. policy for the Iraqi people.

It seems clear that an Iraqi population battered by decades of war, severely deprived under sanctions and highly dependent on government rations and a fragile public health system is at greater risk of a humanitarian disaster than ever before. It is with these considerations in mind that we must be critical of a policy that seeks regime change and the military invasion needed to achieve this goal.

Notes

1 In 1998, the World Health Organization (WHO) reported that each month, between 5,000 and 6,000 Iraqi children died because of sanctions. A 1993 UNICEF report states that there has been a resurgence of vaccine-preventable diseases in Iraq, including polio, diphtheria, and measles. In 1997, UNICEF reported that more than 1.2 million people, including 750,000 children below the age of five, have died because of the scarcity of food and medicine.

2 Relevant sections of International Humanitarian Law, including: The International Convention on Civil and Political Rights, International Convention of Economic and Social Rights, The Geneva Conventions and the Rome Statute of the International Criminal Court.

3 Relevant international standards that apply to refugees and displaced persons include: The 1951 Geneva Convention Relating to the Status of Refugees and the 1967 Protocol Relating to the Status of Refugees (the Refugee Convention), and the Conclusions adopted by the Executive Committee (ExCom) of the UN High Commissioner for Refugees.

Sources

Ahtisaari, Mart. *United Nations Report to the Secretary-General on Humanitarian Needs in Kuwait and Iraq in the Immediate Post-Crisis Environment*, 1991.

Ali, Mohamed, and Iqbal Shah. "Sanctions and Childhood Mortality in Iraq." *The Lancet* 355 (27 May 2000): 1851–57. See *Medact* at www.medact.org.

Centre for Economic and Social Rights. *The Human Cost of War in Iraq*, February 2003. A summary is available at http://www.reliefweb.int/library/documents/2003/cesr-irq-13jan.pdf.

Harding, Luke. *The Observer*, 16 February 2003.

Hoskins, Eric. "Public Health and the Persian Gulf War." In Barry Levy and Victor Sidel, eds., *War and Public Health*. Oxford: Oxford University Press, 1997.

Iraqi Refugees, Asylum Seeker, and Displaced Persons: Current Conditions and Concerns in the Event of War. Human Rights Watch Briefing Paper, February 2003.

International Study Team. *Health and Welfare in Iraq After the Gulf Crisis – An Independent Assessment*, Harvard University, 1991.

International Study Team. *Our Common Responsibility: The Impact of a New War on Iraq's Children*, 30 January 2003.

Lake, Eli J. "U.S. Plans for post-Saddam Iraqi Government." *The Washington Times*, 5 June 2002.

Medcat. "Collateral Damage: The Health and Environmental Costs of War on Iraq," 12 November 2002. See *Medact* at www.medact.org.

Nagy, Thomas. "The Secret Behind the Sanctions: How the U.S. Intentionally Destroyed Iraq's Water Supply." *The Progressive*, September 2001. http://www.progressive.org/0801issue/nagy0901.html.

Oxfam International. Briefing Paper: Protecting Iraq's Civilians, February 2003.

Oxfam International. Briefing Paper: Iraq: Humanitarian-Military Relations, March 2003.

United Nations. UN Security Council Resolution 986, 14 April 1995.

United Nations. UN Security Council Resolution 687, 3 April 1991.

United Nations. UN Security Council Resolution 705, 15 August 1991.

United Nations. UN Confidential Documents. Likely Humanitarian Scenarios, 10 December 2002. http://www.casi.org.uk/info/undocs/war021210.pdf.

United Nations. The Office of the Iraq Program Oil for Food. Report to the Secretary-General pursuant to Paragraphs 7 and 8 of the Security Council Resolution 1409, 12 November 2002.

United Nations. UN Security Council "Humanitarian Panel," 30 March 1999.

United Nations Children's Fund (Unicef). *The Situation of Children in Iraq*, 2002.

United States of America (Senate). U.S. Senate Committee Report, 25 May and 7 October 1994.

United States of America (Congress). Congressional Record: 20 September 2002 (Senate), pp. S8987-S8998.

U.S. Air Force. *Strategic Attack: Air Force Doctrine Document* (20 May 1998): 2–12.

Von Sponeck, H.C. Graf. "Iraq: International Sanctions and What Next?" *Middle East Policy* (October 2000). http://www.afsc.org/iraq/guide/sponeck.shtm

THE WAR ON IRAQ, THE BUSH DOCTRINE AND CANADA'S FUTURE

Jim Harding

Background to the War on Iraq

"We have seen the enemy, and the enemy is us." — *Pogo*

The Anglo-American "coalition" which pre-emptively attacked Iraq has been involved in Iraq's affairs from its beginnings. The Kingdom of Iraq was created under the control of the United Kingdom in 1921, after the fall of the Ottoman Empire. Iraq became a separate country in 1932; however the Iraq Petroleum Co. (IPC), and the Euro-Americans who benefited from cheap oil industrialization, continued to dominate the country.

The Republic of Iraq came into existence in 1958, after the "constitutional" monarchy was overthrown by a nationalist coalition. The new Iraqi leader, General Kassem, immediately faced strong pressure from the United States. Kassem wanted Iraq to become neutral in the Cold War. However, wanting a compliant, not neutral, state, the United States created an invasion plan with its ally Turkey on the pretence of an ensuing "communist take-over."[1] Soviet influence in the region apparently tempered this initiative. The United States then funded Iraqi Kurds and backed a failed assassination attempt on Kassem in 1960.[2]

Saddam Hussein was involved in this botched assassination and went into exile in Cairo. Due to his anti-communism, and his desire to oust the Kassem regime, he and the CIA began to co-operate.[3] When Iraq formed its own oil company in 1962, U.S. opposition deepened. When Kassem began to talk of Iraq's legitimate historical claim to oil-rich Kuwait, "regime change" came quickly. In 1963 the CIA, and British intelligence, backed a coup that overthrew and murdered Kassem and saw thousands of "leftists" and trade unionists killed. The new regime gave assurances it would not nationalize the IPC, which had major U.S. ownership, nor make claims on Kuwait.

After a series of unstable coalitions and coups, the Baath Party took power in 1968. Saddam Hussein became vice–president in charge of oil and quickly emerged as the strong man.[4] The IPC was nationalized in 1972, and Iraq began to modernize in hope of becoming the uncontested leader of the Arab world.

The U.S-backed, Shah of Iran, was deposed in 1979. The Iranian revolution was a call for Muslims everywhere to create Islamic states, which was a clear threat to the oil-monarchies which were U.S. "allies." After the Iranian "revolution," Hussein staged a successful "palace coup" and moved to establish absolute power in Iraq.

Though Iraq was an emerging secular nation, it was still dominated by Sunni Muslims in a country, like Iran, with a Shi'i majority.[5] The Iranian regime was therefore seen as doubly threatening to Hussein's hold over Iraq.[6] Thinking that Iran's internal chaos might enable Iraq to win back land lost in a 1975 agreement, Iraq invaded Iran in 1980.

The United States, which wanted to defeat Khomeni's theocracy at any human cost, backed Iraq. There were eight years of vicious warfare, reminiscent of the brutality of World War I trenches. Oil revenues went to profit the merchants of death, rather than to meet desperate humans needs.[7] It was "oil for weapons," not "oil for food." With nearly a million young, conscripted soldiers dead, and still no victor, a cease-fire was finally brokered by the UN in 1988.

Saddam Hussein earned his reputation for cruelty after his regime's use of chemical, and perhaps biological, weapons during this war. What is ignored in the U.S.'s demonization of Hussein, is that from 1985, and perhaps earlier, until 1989, U.S. companies legally exported the materials required for Iraq to develop these weapons. This included anthrax, as well as other biological toxins. U.S. exports also included "precursors" for chemical weapons, like nerve gas, and equipment for chemical warheads. Later, in 1994, a U.S. Senate Committee found that the biological materials "were identical to those the U.N. inspectors found and removed."[8]

After the chemical slaughter of five thousand Iraqi Kurds in 1988, the U.S. Congress passed legislation to stop U.S. exports of these materials to Iraq. However, the Reagan-controlled White House, which had built up the military resources of Hussein's regime, vetoed it. The analogy with the origins of al-Qaeda, which the Reagan administration had armed to fight the Soviet army in Afghanistan, is astonishing.[9]

In the build-up to the 2003 invasion of Iraq, there was much rhetoric about the extreme violence of Hussein's regime. However, if ending violence were the core motivation to invade Iraq, these Western rulers would have had to have had a major conversion from their past embracing of violence in the service of national and corporate interest. Through its support of coups and assassinations to protect Cold War and oil interests, the United States and Britain contributed to the political culture of violence within which Saddam rose to power.

"Don't try to put out a fire by throwing on more fire. Don't wash a wound with blood." — Rumi

If, in the aftermath of this war, we are to gain a deeper commitment to international peace and security through international law, rather than head further down the path of pre-emptive warfare, we must cast a wide net of understanding over recent events. Though sanctioned by the UN, it is naive to look for simple, righteous motives in the 1991 Gulf War. Iraq's invasion of Kuwait, and breach of the UN Charter, was rooted in pan-Arab nationalism, a desire to expand into this oil-rich area, and the vulnerability of Iraq as nearly completely land-locked.

But the invasion was triggered by a specific crisis. After the ravages of the Iran–Iraq war, Iraq became dependent on the financial backing of both Kuwait and Saudi Arabia. In 1990 these countries sold Iraq's debts to international banks. When Kuwait later flooded the oil market, further cutting demand for cash-strapped Iraq, a summit was called to try to negotiate a settlement. When this failed, Iraq invaded Kuwait.[10]

After the Gulf War, the United States strengthened its military presence in Kuwait, which became the launching pad for its later attack on Iraq. It will remain one of the great examples of "big power" double standards in the Middle East that war was declared on Iraq by a U.S.-UN coalition, for illegally crossing the Kuwait border in 1991, while the United States and Britain, without UN backing, and breaching the UN Charter, crossed the same border, in the other direction, to start the 2003 war on Iraq.

In the Vietnam War, and the Gulf War, and now the war on Iraq, the United States perpetrated falsehoods to create an image of it intervening to right a wrong and to protect a victim of aggression.[11] This "good versus evil" story, evolving from Protestant frontierism into Cold War, superpower ideology is so imbedded in the American mythology that it is very difficult for most Americans to see any larger truth.[12] It is revealing that the Afro-American population, evolving from U.S. slavery, is the major exception.

After forty-three days of smart-bombing, and "collateral" and ecological carnage in 1991, Iraq became subject to UN arms inspection and sanctions.[13] This persisted until 1997, when Iraq barred inspectors. Though Russia brokered a compromise for renewed inspections, Iraq again stopped inspections in early 1998, accusing the U.S.-led team of spying. In February 1998, UN Secretary General Kofi Annan re-negotiated inspections, but in October Iraq stopped working with UNSCOM. In November, Iraq reconsidered, and UNSCOM returned. Then, in December UNSCOM's new head, American Richard Butler, reported that Iraq was refusing to co-operate. Soon after, the UN ordered all inspectors to leave, and U.S. air strikes on Iraq immediately began.

In its 2002–2003 propaganda, the Bush (Jr.) administration seriously distorted this chronology to make it look like Iraq stopped inspections, outright, and this was done to hide weapons of mass destruction (WMD), which might get into the hands of hostile terrorists.[14] Actually, there was a lengthy to-and-fro of negotiations before inspections ended. The larger context for the inspection process included the devastating effects of the UN sanctions, mostly on children; a CIA-backed attempt to assassinate Hussein, the escalation of unsanctioned U.S. bombing in the "no fly" zones, and the growing fear that U.N.-enforced disarmament was a prelude to a U.S. invasion.[15] It has been recently revealed in the media that the Iraqi government's last-minute efforts to appease the U.S. just prior to the invasion were rebuffed, obviously because the U.S. countdown to war had begun. It was invasion and occupation that the U.S. was interested in and not compliance.

Americans woke up to the conflict, in 1998, when U.N. inspectors left Iraq. Except for a few American "moralists," who complained of the dying of more than 1.5 million Iraqis due to the sanctions, the U.S. population had no interest in Iraq until after Bush took power and the catastrophe of 9/11.[16] In the aftermath, and Bush's "war on terrorism," the U.S. public was feeling particularly patriotic and vulnerable. In this context, past UNSCOM Chief Richard Butler told a U.S. Senate Committee that Iraq was still producing chemical and biological weapons and might be developing nuclear weapons.[17] The unlikelihood of these charges, which was already documented, was immaterial. The rhetoric of fear and aggression was ratcheted up. The "war on terrorism" and war on Iraq were collapsed into one policy. At one point, over 50 per cent of Americans mistakenly believed Hussein was behind 9/11 and had nuclear weapons.[18]

In late September 2002, the United States proposed a UN resolution with strict new inspection rules, which Iraq rejected. However, a month later Hans Blix, the chief UN weapons inspector, and Iraq agreed on new inspection arrangements, but U.S. Secretary of State Colin Powell rejected these. In retrospect, with what we now know, by then the United States was after UN support to legitimize its decision to go to war. However, Bush was already saying the United States didn't really need UN authorization, and could take pre-emptive action in self-defence. This, however, would contravene the UN Charter, go against international law, and would not likely be acceptable to European allies. British Prime Minister Blair, already in deep trouble with rising anti-war sentiment, desperately wanted this UN legitimacy. The UN and the United States were on a collision course.

After failing to convince the world that Iraq was linked to 9/11 terrorism, the United States refocused its attack on Iraq having WMD. On 8 November 2002, the UN Security Council unanimously approved a compromise resolution (Resolution 1441) calling for Iraq to completely disarm or face "serious consequences." Several knowledgeable sources had already questioned whether Iraq indeed still had any WMD. This included past UN inspector Scott Ritter – an ex-Marine Republican, whose dissent against Bush's propaganda machine laid much of the groundwork for the pre-war, anti-war movement.[19] It also included political refugee Hussein Kamel, who had previously headed Iraq's WMD program and was assassinated by the Hussein regime when he returned to Iraq.[20] Thinking people worldwide were having trouble swallowing the shifting mix of justifications for war.

UN inspection reports initially were fairly ambiguous and provided "ammunition" for both poles forming in the Security Council. But, by the time of the 14 March 2003 Security Council meeting, a pattern that didn't satisfy the United States was taking shape. The U.S. and British case was already greatly weakened when it was found that an earlier British intelligence report, submitted to the February Security Council meeting, arguing Iraq had WMD, was largely plagiarized. Then, at the Summit of 116 Non-Aligned countries, held 25 February, there was unanimous opposition to war without Security Council authorization. Later, both the Arab Summit and the Islamic Summit opposed any pre-emptive war. All the time, anti-war demonstrations continued to grow worldwide.[21]

Then, on March 7th, Hans Blix reported to the Security Council that he "welcomed the acceleration of initiative" on the part of Iraq since January. He reported that Iraq was starting to be "proactive," even if it wasn't "immediately co-operative." There were clearly more tasks left to verify that all chemical and biological weapons materials and capacities were accounted for, and destroyed, and disarmament complete. But he stressed, with only three months of inspections to date, that "disarmament and verification can't be instant." At that meeting IAEA head Mohamed El Baradei also reported that a document that Iraq had imported uranium to enrich for nuclear weapons was forged. That President Bush Jr. had referred to this falsehood as fact in his January 2003 State of the Union address came back to haunt and discredit the U.S. administration.[22]

Rather than agreeing to intensify inspections and establish a schedule for key remaining items, as was suggested by other Security Council members, the United States and Britain pressed ahead to try to get UN support for war. Colin Powell argued in vain that "serious consequences" had always meant war. Then the Anglo-American coalition floated an amendment placing a March 17th deadline on Iraqi compliance to Resolution 1441. France, and later Russia, however, said they would veto this. More significant, the six undecided, small countries on the Security Council, did not budge. The resistance of Latin American countries, with an intimate history of U.S. foreign policies encouraging political violence, was particularly significant.[23]

The United States rejected a six-country proposal to extend the deadline for Iraq to March 31st, which was being supported behind the scenes by Canada as a compromise motion.[24] Then, under growing British pressure for a second resolution, Tony Blair floated six demands that Iraq had to meet or face war. One British cabinet minister referred to Blair as "reckless," and on March 17th, Robin Cook resigned as Blair's House Leader because of the illegality of the coming war. The same day, the United States and Britain withdrew their second resolution, rather than have it go down to defeat. Bush stated "the time for diplomacy is over," and the war machine went into full gear. There was little doubt left that the decision to go to war had been made before all the diplomatic jostling. A credible explanation of continued U.S. involvement in UN diplomacy until 17 March is that war preparations were not fully ready.[25]

The Bush Doctrine's Threat to International Peace and Security

"There is no way to peace. Peace is the way." – Gandhi

After 9/11 Bush became the ideologue of Pax Americana. He polarized political discourse, in a fashion similar to anti-communism and McCarthyism. He talked threateningly of how "either you are with us or you are with the terrorists," and how those who "harboured" anyone the United States considered terrorists were now also enemies of the United States[26] Speaking of a "crusade" against terrorism, and invoking his revengeful, Protestant, fundamentalist "god" into the language of war, he became the "cowboy evangelist." All this fear mongering and manufacturing of consent, of course, was in the name of American-style "freedom." Bush's phrase, "the axis of evil," for which Canada's *National Post* columnist David Frum takes some credit, instantly put international politics back a half-century. Bush's simplistic, retributive approach to justice has no room for the intricacies of international law or peacemaking. If anything, it stimulates conflict that can lead to warfare.[27] The transparency of Bush's mixing of religion and nationalism into belligerent superpower rhetoric is likely what catalyzed the pre-war anti-war movement throughout the world.

A major influence on the creation of the Bush doctrine was the writings of *Atlantic Monthly* journalist and author Robert Kaplan.[28] His book, *The Coming Anarchy*, in particular, spoke to the fears and aspirations of these men.[29] Kaplan's most recent book, coming out with the neo-Reaganites already controlling the Pentagon, is appropriately named *Warrior Politics*. The subtitle, "Why Leadership Demands a Pagan Ethos," implicitly advances the violence of raw power associated with many forms of paganism. The attraction to this image shows you how far astray the fundamentalist "Christianity" associated with the Republican right is from the original Christians, who preached love and peace, and equality under a common God. The underlying perspective is more like that attributed to the Roman Empire, which repressed the early Christians, and the Holy Roman Empire, which turned Christianity into a repressive and colonial ideology.

It is not surprising that Kaplan's writings are so appealing to many Americans, in their present circumstance. Thinking they had won the Cold War but, after 9/11, being psychologically shell-shocked and forced out of their "consumption and celebrity-worshipping bubble," they have had to quickly "grow up" to face the realization that history hadn't really ended with the "Corporate American Dream."

But, there are many risks in Kaplan constructing such an eclectic worldview out of bits and pieces of political philosophy, with complete disregard for historical context. Perhaps this is what happens when the American far right, so traditionally hostile to serious intellectual endeavour, ran out of simplistic, dualistic direction and purpose in the aftermath of the Cold War.[30] It is now grasping around for "new ideas" to justify asserting global American hegemony. Of course, these aren't really new ideas. They are the ideas of authoritarian elitism, which are linked to the rise of fascism in Europe.[31] The similarity is one main reason that people from "old Europe" have – almost instinctively – been repelled by the Bush doctrine.

Kaplan makes a lot out of NATO's intervention in Bosnia, as an example of a "global constabulary force to intervene in human tragedies." He argued that "as Bosnia showed, such a force is more likely to emerge from NATO than from the UN."[32] Not quite. In the aftermath of the War on Iraq, not only is the UN being sidelined by the United States, but

NATO is now deeply divided and unlikely to again throw its lot in with the United States so readily.

But, even though Kaplan cannot see the implications of the practices he is advocating, he provides a "good" rationale for them. As if intended as a memo to Bush, he writes:

> *Because international goals are best realized through national self-interest, the President of the U.S. should project power through the UN to the benefit of both. The U.S. should in essence, without declaring it, take over the UN in order to make it a transparent multiplier of American and western power.*[33]

Well, there it is. The outcomes were not quite what was predicted. The UN has not rolled over to the United States, though it will be relegated to a secondary role in post-war Iraq. The UN, and international peace and security, certainly hasn't "benefited" from the U.S.'s arbitrary use of power. And the United States, with Britain at its side, has had to "multiply" its power pretty much all by itself.

Canada and a New World Order

"No blood for oil" – anti-war slogan

This slogan has been used in anti-war marches throughout the world. Even before the war started, half of polled Canadians thought oil was a factor in the U.S. plan to attack Iraq. Not only is Bush, and many of his cohorts, schooled in the oil industry; the U.S. economy will increasingly become dependent on oil imports. Achieving geopolitical, superpower supremacy, and controlling security of supply of oil are inextricably linked, though a move toward renewable energies and self-sufficiency could alter this.

A decade ago, when the neo-Reaganites were forming their policies, the trend-line was clear. The bulk of global oil production and oil reserves were in areas of actual or potential political destabilization, often due to resistance to Western globalization. In 1993, countries at high risk for political instability had 25 per cent of known oil reserves. And, very telling, Iraq had the most of any of these countries, with 10 per cent of the world's total. Next was Iran, with 9 per cent. When you added in moderate-risk countries, it included 90 per cent of the world's known reserves. Saudi Arabia had the largest percentage of world oil reserves in this group, at 26 per cent.[34]

The United States, as the most oil-consuming country on the planet, is interested in maintaining or gaining a direct say in the politics and economics of Saudi Arabia, Iraq, and Iran because they have nearly 50 per cent of the world's oil reserves. Iraq is the most strategic base for this, bordering both Saudi Arabia and Iran. It may sound crude, but "democracy" is becoming an American superpower code word for stable, accessible oil. The continued priority of oil over democracy is shown clearly in the aftermath of the 1991 Gulf War; which too was promoted as a war of liberation. After the "liberation of Kuwait" there was no demand by the United States to create democracy in that country. And the war to "democratize" Iraq was primarily launched from this non-democratic, U.S. client state. After Iraq is within U.S. control, based on the neo-Reaganites own pronouncements, it is likely it will house a new military base, to enhance its influence on the whole region, and perhaps to launch a Pax Americana offensive on Iran.[35]

"War for oil" politics continues to unfold. Since 1993, huge oil reserves, larger than those in Saudi Arabia, have been located by Russia in the Black and Caspian seas. This oil was becoming an alternative source for both Germany and France, and until the war over Kosovo, it could be piped directly through Europe. After 1999, it was piped through the Caucasus Mountains, through Iraq to the Persian Gulf port of Basra. What may be helping to consolidate the Anglo-American military alliance in Iraq, is the British Petroleum–Standard Oil merger in 1998.[36] The oil interests of what is now the largest global oil multinational, along with a fear of Saddam starting oil fires, may help explain why controlling Basra, and the northern pipeline facilities at Kirkuk and Mosul, was such a military priority. The United States will watch the Kurds and Turks closely to see that they don't use the war on Iraq as an excuse to assert their own control in this oil-rich area.

This opens up a complex can of worms about oil, colonialism, and war. U.S. oil companies directly benefited from France's defeat in Vietnam in 1954 and in Algeria in 1962. And the United States not only didn't support France in either case but helped arm the Vietnamese at the end of World War II. You can see why France may be thinking there is a pattern. Chevron is now the oil partner to Vietnam, and Texaco-Mobile-Chevron is the oil partner to Algeria. It now looks like France (and Germany and Russia) may be about to lose out to BP in Iraq.[37]

The Iraqi people, like all people plundered for the resources of colonialism and industrialism, know full well that oil is a mixed blessing. One Iraqi saying refers to oil as "the excrement of the devil." Not only did the struggle for oil keep Iraqis under external colonial rule for nearly half a century, but under internal authoritarian repression. For a short period in the 1970s, it looked like the nationalization of oil might fund a modern, secular, and possibly democratic society in Iraq. However, the Iran–Iraq war nullified that. It was Hussein's near absolute power over oil and the country's distorted development based on militarization and dependence on oil that enabled him to consolidate power and posture as a megalomaniac.

After Iraq's defeat in the Gulf War, UN sanctions on oil exports placed Iraqi people in a new and, for some, deadly vulnerability. Now they are being promised a new era of oil-based wealth, by their U.S. and British liberator-conquerors. But we know this will mean another highly stratified, class-based society, of a few haves and mostly have-nots. Before the war was even over, U.S. corporations were taking over managing some of Iraqi's infrastructure. U.S. corporations will be the primary benefactors of the profitable, post-war reconstruction. There is a serious threat that the UN's role may be reduced to creating legitimacy. The lack of UN authority in post-war Iraq will surely exacerbate the humanitarian and political crisis.

Military and economic power go hand in hand with the United States, and they both depend on oil.[38] The oil-guzzling U.S. economy dwarfs all others in the world, with a GDP in 2000 of $9.8 trillion.[39] Not even the integration of all European economies in the EC, with a total GDP of $7.9 trillion, comes close to the United States. Only Japan, as another single country economy, with a GDP of $4.7 trillion, stands out in comparison with the United States. The Canadian economy, with a GDP of $717 billion, is only the size of the state of Texas, the political homeland of George Bush Jr.

The annual U.S. military budget of $400 billion is now greater than the total Russian GDP of $259 billion. To get some perspective on the magnitude of the U.S. war machine that invaded Iraq, this figure is about three hundred times Iraq's annual military budget in the post 1991 period. In the three weeks it took for the United States to get to and enter Baghdad, there were over thirty thousand aerial bombs or missiles dropped on Iraq. Many thousands more were delivered by low-flying helicopters and tanks. Were these kinds of resources available to meet human needs, some fundamental international peace and security would be forthcoming.[40] But the Bush regime considers that "utopian internationalism." Under the Bush Doctrine, brute force is the means to gain and keep respect and honour. And, of course, to control oil and oil profits.

The obscene magnitude of the killing power of the United States and the willingness to use this for global domination of resources should worry all people in the world. As the geographic neighbour of this gigantic, and increasingly aggressive military-industrial power, Canada and Canadians are now particularly challenged. We are seeing a warfare, not a welfare, state re-emerging south of our border. Warfare policies are deeply interlocked with the dynamics of American economic growth. This affects the nature of technological innovation, of the social structure and stratification, as well as the perpetuation of social and domestic violence.[41]

If we are interested in strengthening international law and peace and security, we have to confront this underlying link between the economy, warfare, and violence. The *Report on Business* "Shock and Awe" edition referred to a study of the relationship between U.S. economic booms and profit-taking and major military and geopolitical crises since World War II.[42] In all but one case (i.e., the Berlin Blockade of 1948), there was substantial growth in, and profits from, stocks in the aftermath of these crises. Taking the average gains of the Dow Jones, if investors bought during the "gloom" of such a crisis, one year later they had earned substantial amounts. The increases were 29 per cent from the Korean War, 34 per cent after the Cuban missile crisis, and 24 per cent after the 1991 Gulf War.

This is what the Bush administration is hoping for in the aftermath of this war. In fall 2002, with Bush's ratings starting to decline, after peaking in the wake of 9/11, and concerns about the U.S. economy not rebounding from the recession, launching and quickly winning the war against Iraq was becoming both a political and economic necessity. The uncertainty around the build-up to war, the projections of a massive $1.8 trillion government deficit, greatly due to a further $700 billion projected tax cuts, and increasing military spending, were not creating a climate conducive to investment.[43] One reason the Bush administration wasn't willing to let multilateral processes go on any longer was because of the need to get this war "over" and hope for an economic recovery, prior to the fall 2004 presidential election.

"Oh Canada, [do] we stand on guard for thee?"

Opponents of Mulroney's Free Trade Agreement (FTA) warned that, with even greater dependency on the U.S. market, it would become much more difficult to maintain an independent Canadian foreign policy. They also warned that continental "free trade" may threaten domestic policies, such as Medicare. In the aftermath of the Chrétien Liberals' not supporting the United States and Britain in their war on Iraq, we heard a barrage of rhetoric from the Alliance Party, oil baron Premier Klein, and other business interests concerned about U.S. economic retribution. In other words, Canada should have supported the United States in its superpower adventures, regardless of international law because we are a branch-plant. They would have us reduced to the status and stature of a Kuwait.[44]

There is no disputing we're increasingly a branch-plant. The percentage of GDP which Canada exports has grown since the FTA and is now at 45 per cent. This is the greatest amount of any industrial nation. And, more telling, the vast amount of this (88%) goes to the United States. This means that the United States buys 38 per cent of everything Canada produces. Contrast this with the U.S. relationship to us. With the largest domestic consumer market in the world, the United

States only exports 13 per cent of its GDP. And only 22 per cent of this goes to Canada. This means that only 3 per cent of what the United States produces is bought by Canada.[45]

You can see who needs whom. In the name of post-9/11 homeland security, and/or as punishment for Canada not being a superpower cheerleader, the U.S.-Canada border could be steadily tightened. And, whereas Canada's economy has become more vulnerable to such trade interruptions, the U.S. economy doesn't desperately require our market. While it does require our natural resources, these could be secured through a combination of foreign ownership, and even relocating companies south of the border, for easy access to the large U.S. market.

This is big bargaining power. The United States might not even need troops in Canada to secure superpower supremacy here. Its huge economic weapon might coerce us to spend even more on the military, as part of an integrated coalition for future wars. These integrated forces might, in a future scenario, even repress "rebellious" Canadian citizens. The United States might also coerce us to create a continental policing and security system and to harmonize our refugee and immigration policies.

The anti-free trade scenario of the decline of Canada was, however, too economically deterministic.[46] It often failed to see the military and imperial side of Corporate America. But, in the aftermath of the war on Iraq, we can more easily imagine the depth of the threat to our future. One thing of which we can be sure is that, as long as the Alliance Party and its successor the Conservative Party has significant parliamentary power, it will be the Trojan Horse pushing for these Pax Americana policies.

But Canada did not buckle under the immense pressure exerted on it to support the war on Iraq. From the beginning of the UN crisis, through the huge anti-war marches, right up to the start of the war, Canadian public opinion held at about two-thirds opposed to unilateral, unsanctioned action. A drop in anti-war sentiment after the war began wasn't unexpected. The federal Liberals were trying to straddle the "war on terrorism," which they still supported in the Gulf, and the war on Iraq, which they weren't supporting. The term "allies" has powerful, emotional connotations in our military and Cold War history and identity. The phrase "turning our backs on our American friends," touches deep visceral feelings about loyalty and even self-worth. Some Canadians may sing "God Bless America" at a Toronto Blue Jays game, or sing the American national anthem at an Ottawa or Alberta pro-war rally, thinking it is a sign of respect for our American neighbours. If you try to imagine Americans singing "Oh Canada," you will, however, realize that deep continentalist and imperial forces are at play. When criticizing Canada for not joining the "coalition," America's current ambassador described Canada as "part of our family," saying that the United States would be there for Canada if Canada were threatened. Does this mean he sees Canadians as gullible junior partners, i.e., adopted children, in the American Empire? Of course, we aren't one big American family. And it can be very manipulative to collapse the distinction between countries, and, more vital, between state and family. This latter distinction is as crucial to democratic theory and practice as the separation of church and state. The irrational passion that can come from connecting the identity of family and state is shown in all authoritarian regimes; including Nazi Germany, when Hitler, the Führer, became the "father" of the nation and "race."[47]

The neo-Reaganites, like their neo-conservative allies in the Alliance Party, have consistently manipulated the language of family into a return to patriarchal values in a new American collectivism. The gated suburb, under threat from crime, is now becoming the gated nation, under threat from terrorists.

Under Pax Americana, being part of Ambassador Cellucci's one big American family, we would come to live within an umbrella of fear, and ultimately aggression.

However, the drop in support for the no-war position in Canada is as much about the economic impact as outright identification with the U.S. position. Cellucci has also used his position to fan these fears. He has implied their will be repercussions, and at the same time, he used the occasion of this foreign policy split, and Canada's economic dependence to further advance the Bush administration's goal of a continental energy market.

Only Britain significantly supported the U.S. war effort. The flimsy nature of the larger "coalition of the willing" shows how little global support there is for Pax Americana. The fact that much of Europe put resisting American expansionism over and above preserving unity in the EC and in NATO shows that this is likely a watershed in world affairs. Geo-political reconfiguration, a new world order not under American hegemony in this post-Cold War era, may be underway. It is not far-fetched that even corporate-backed "globalization" may be being put at risk by Bush's "warrior politics."

Mexico is even more vulnerable to U.S. economic retribution than Canada, and even though they were on the Security Council, they didn't crack. And if we look at other countries with huge economic ties to the United States (with the exception of Britain, with its own historical interest in Iraq), they stayed clear of the Bush doctrine. Canada was not alone as a major U.S. trading partner in not supporting this war. Not only was worldwide public opinion solidly against this war; so too were most of the U.S. trading partners and its traditional allies.

Just why Canada ended up in this position of opposition to the war on Iraq is perhaps our most crucial question. Certainly our fragile heritage as a welfare and not a warfare state is part of the answer. So, too, is our important role in the history of international law, the UN, and peacekeeping, and a heritage of independent foreign policy in Suez, Vietnam, and now. Although we are "caught" between the two Anglo-American empires, our multi-national character interconnects us with Europe, and even with France. The juxtaposition of a more internationalist Quebec, with the more continentalist West, is a vital moderator on the pressures to give in to Pax Americana. Oil wealth, as in Alberta, apparently plays a role in the flow of ideology, here, as well as in Iraq.

The potential of a constitutional and cultural reconciliation with First Nations and Metis also affects the flow of ideas that shape who we are, and who we can become. Communitarian Aboriginal traditions are helping to stimulate the broader Canadian society to consider "restorative" perspectives on seeking justice, which could help us break out of the cycle of punishment, revenge, and further violence, which is so evident to the south.

But we could continue to slide towards continental economic and military integration. The refusal to join the war on Iraq is therefore an opportunity and challenge to shore up our vulnerabilities, to deepen our commitments and resolve, and to build new bridges between diverse peoples and persons here and abroad. There is no hope or new direction in the destruction and threats resulting from the Bush Doctrine. We need Canadian alternatives, which respect the interconnections between ecology, justice, and peace, which put means squarely in the service of ends.

Postscript: The Future in Iraq and the United States

"We're flying blind on this." — U.S. intelligence officer

Though the U.S. troops initially avoided the feared urban warfare, and the Hussein regime fell quickly, the celebration of victory was short-lived. Within days, the "liberated" were expressing opposition to the U.S. occupation. First through demonstrations and later through guerrilla attacks, Iraqi opposition to occupation accelerated to the point that during the first six months of occupation, more American military were killed in attacks than during the war.

The military might of the United States just couldn't make the transition to creating public order. Things went from bad to worse. Looting and arson were rampant. And through the chaos, U.S. priorities became more transparent. Only the ministries of oil and information, and not even the world-renowned Baghdad Museum of Antiquities, received any protection.

The credibility of the U.S. regime continued to slip. Soon General Garner had to be replaced by Paul Bremer, a loyal neo-Reaganite. Though he moved to quickly establish a Council of co-operative Iraqis, the steady killing of U.S. soldiers continued. Water, electricity, and hospital services were still not restored months into the occupation.

Ironically, the United States and Britain had to go back to the UN to get the oil embargo lifted. Security Council members who opposed the war bargained hard for three weeks to get some accountability for the use of oil revenues for reconstruction. (USAID is providing $1 billion of lucrative contracts, mostly to U.S. corporations.) However, the occupiers were left fully responsible for ensuing conditions, which was probably the best the UN could salvage from the fiasco. The UN may yet come out stronger, not weaker, from this crisis.

The debate about the new "American Empire" went more mainstream in the homeland. Some called for the United States to act like an empire and create a more imperial-like military and civil service. Others speculated that the quagmire the United States seemed to be moving into was symptomatic of imperial "overreach," and perhaps even a sign that the empire was actually waning.

That there were no WMD, which was the biggest pretence for the invasion, continued to chip away at public opinion in the United States and Britain. The Blair government has faced the greatest crisis in the short-run, especially after the suicide of David Kelly, a government advisor on Iraq, who apparently gave the BBC a secret interview on the tampering of intelligence documents to exaggerate the threat of Iraq to justify the war. If the Blair government should ultimately fall, it will be a strong sign to other government's that backing U.S. unilateralism is politically risky. And that would put the Bush Doctrine more on the defensive at home.

Bush has already looked like a hunted man. Though he tried to recast his presidency, with his "roadmap to peace" in the Middle East, he was journalistically hounded after revelations that CIA intelligence information, used in his pre-war State of the Union address about Iraq importing uranium from Niger, was knowingly erroneous.

But the litany of official untruths about the war still grows. Private Jessica Lynch was manufactured into a national war hero, after it was alleged she was injured and captured in battle and freed by U.S. marine's in a heroic night raid. It turned out she was injured in a vehicle accident, given medical care by an Iraqi doctor, and rescued without resistance. That, however, didn't stop the U.S. military granting her the Purple Heart and Bronze Star as well as prisoner-of-war medal.[48] As U.S.

casualties continue to mount, there are signs of low morale and public discontent among the fighting forces in Iraq. As recruits and reservists begin to fear for their lives, and are no longer mesmerized by the heroic self-image of "freedom-fighters," deserting might return as a political force, as it was during Vietnam.

Suggesting some desperation, there is now talk of "internationalizing" the occupying force. To do this the United States would have to go back to the UN, and possibly the EC, which it shirked in the first place, and give up more of its control. This would be tantamount to the war opponents rescuing the Empire. For the present, the United States is creating an army of Iraqis to try to buffer itself from the deep opposition to its presence. The United States had hoped that the killing of Hussein's two sons in July 2003 would be a turning point in the war of resistance. Even after the capture of Saddam Hussein, resistance continues. This war may yet humiliate the neo-Reaganites in search of Pax America, and encourage intimidated domestic voices, who would prefer the United States to be more of a multilateral partner in world affairs.

Most compelling to those in search of a stable, just peace in the region, the innocent casualties of the U.S.-led "war on terrorism," used to justify the war on Iraq in the aftermath of 9/11 have already outstripped those of "terrorism" itself. That this is not a viable or acceptable foreign policy will continue to sink in, in both Iraq and America.

Notes

1   William Blum, *Rogue State: A Guide to the World's Only Superpower* (Monro, Maine: Common Courage Press, 2000), 134.

2   Some sources say 1959. See Richard Sale, "Saddam Key in Early CIA Plot," *Straight Goods* (12 April 2003).

3 Hussein's anti-communism and identification with Stalin were not contradictory, as the Bolsheviks found out. This political background was discussed in the documentary "The Long Road to War," *The Passionate Eye*, CBC television, 18 March 2003.

4 Albert Hourani, *A History of the Arab Peoples* (Cambridge, MA: Harvard University Press, 1991), 417.

5 Colonial powers often left minority ethnic groups, to which they had given preferred status and advantage, in neo-colonial authority. We saw what legacy this can leave in the slaughtering in Rwanda. Creating truly multi-national states, without this neo-colonial legacy, remains one of the major challenges to international peace and security. Canada has not yet reached this goal with its constitutional negotiations with First Nations and Metis.

6 Hourani, *A History of Arab Peoples*, 432.

7 By 1984, Iraq's per capita military spending was the ninth largest in the world. Meanwhile its economic and social standing was only 73rd. The U.S. at the time was eighth in per capita military spending and was already relying on the military might of its "allies" in the region. At the time, oil-rich Saudi Arabia was No. 1, worldwide, in per capita military spending. See Ruth Leger Sivard, *World Military and Social Expenditures – 1987–88* (Washington: World Priorities, 1987), 46–48.

8 Blum, *Rogue State*, 122. Also see reports of U.S. Senate Committee on Banking, Housing and Urban Affairs with Respect to Export Administration (25 May and 7 October 1994).

9 For a discussion of Reagan's training and arming of the Afghan Mujahideen, which included al-Qaeda, see Eqbal Ahmad, *Terrorism: Theirs and Ours* (New York: Seven Stories Press, 2001), 11–26.

10 See the documentary, "Oil in Iraq: Blessing or Curse?," *The Passionate Eye*, CBC television, 26 March 2003.

11 In 1964, an erroneous report was made of a North Vietnamese attack on a U.S. gunship in the Bay of Tonkin, which whipped up aggressive, patriotic sentiment at home. In the case of the Gulf War, there was an erroneous report of an Iraqi attack on a health institution with babies in incubators. In this war in Iraq, the United States has made many false claims, including that Iraq was behind al-Qaeda.

12 Political psychology can be helpful. With his background in oil and Texas subculture (remember the Alamo); his "born again" Protestantism, and even what some claim is his "dry drunk" personality, George Bush Jr. was the "perfect" ideologue for this war. However, it is his absolutist moralism, which flows from the above influences, that has made him so vulnerable to critical journalism.

13 Both Iraq and the U.S.-UN forces share responsibility for this. Hussein's notorious oil-well fires, and the U.S.'s use of depleted uranium (DU) weaponry, both did immense ecological damage.

14 It is most interesting to compare the way CNN and BBC have backgrounded their audiences on this conflict. There are details about the chronology, provided by the BBC, which were never mentioned by CNN. A good reference on the chronology prior to UN resolution 1441, is "Timeline: Iraq Weapons Inspection," BBC.com (18 November 2002).

15 "The Long Road to War," 18 March 2003.

16 This is more than one in twenty of the Iraqi population.

17 BBC.com, Timeline, 2.

18 Ian Brown, "Over a bloody rainbow," *The Globe and Mail* (29 March 2003). In a BBC interview, *Newsweek* journalist, Eleanor Clift, suggested it was two-thirds of Americans at one point.

19 See Scott Ritter, *Endgame* (Simon and Schuster, 1999, 2002), and *War on Iraq* (Profile Books, 2002). Ritter was the head of the U.S.-led UN inspections when they ended in 1998. He couldn't accept Bush Jr's manipulation of the facts and was on talk shows and doing speeches non-stop prior to the war. His debate with Blair at a pre-war Labour Convention further strengthened the anti-war resolve in Britain.

20 This was reported in Norman Soloman "Falling on Deaf Ears," *Prairie Dog* (6 March 2003): 11. Also see John Barry, "The Defector's Secrets," *Newsweek* (3 March 2003).

21 Millions were in the streets worldwide prior to the war even starting. This unprecedented global protest may be a sign of the potential of establishing international law, linked to democratization, and ultimately banning war as a means of national-imperial policy.

22 In July 2003, CIA Director George Tenet admitted the intelligence information used in the president's address that Iraq was trying to import uranium from Niger was erroneous. While this may have been meant to deflect "heat" from Bush, it coincided with his trip to

Africa, and the story became front-page news internationally. There is a growing litany of official U.S. "lies" about the war, which are receiving international attention. See Christopher Scheer, "Lies the White House Told Us," *Prairie Dog* (10 July 2003): 5.

23 Only Columbia ended up giving tacit support to the United States for its war on Iraq.

24 This wasn't much of a compromise, as it might only have postponed war by a week. But that week was vital, as it put Canada on the side of international law.

25 There is growing evidence for this. A week into the war, U.S. military head Tommy Franks admitted the United States had been preparing for this war for a year.

26 This would, literally, put the United States at war with some of its allies, such as Saudi Arabia, the homeland of bin Laden and most of the 9/11 "bombers."

27 Gwynne Dyer, *Ignorant Armies: Sliding into War in Iraq* (Toronto: McClelland & Stewart, 2003).

28 The evolution of this ideology within the Project for the New American Century (PNAC) is discussed in Jim Harding, "Pax Americana," *Briarpatch* (May 2003): 23–24.

29 Robert D. Kaplan, *The Coming Anarchy: Shattering the Dreams of the Post Cold War* (New York: Random House, 2000).

30 The American "right" has typically been hostile to the country's intellectual heritage, preferring to label critically thinking people as "eggheads" rather than to engage in serious inquiry and dialogue. Most neo-conservative think tanks, as with the PNAC, function as ideological training stations.

31 It is noteworthy that, in discussing "the dangers of peace," Kaplan is enamoured with Gaetano Mosca, who helped lay the theoretical foundations for Italian fascism with *The Ruling Class* (New York: McGraw-Hill, 1939).

32 Kaplan, *Coming Anarchy*, 181.

33 Ibid.

34 Benjamin R. Barber, *Jihad vs McWorld: How Globalism and Tribalism are Reshaping the World* (New York: Ballantine, 1996), 44–47.

35 It is too early to tell just how the U.S. occupation of Iraq will unfold. The United States may actually find itself less able to use the Middle East as a military location because of the war and

occupation. Soon after the war, the United States announced it would begin to use its "new European" allies, Bulgaria and Hungary, in Iraq.

36   It still goes under BP.

37   Marshall Smith, "Oil on your French Toast," *Brojan Gazette/* brojan.com (27 March 2003).

38   The military dependence on oil is catastrophic. Sivard estimates that one year of Pentagon oil consumption would fuel the complete public transportation system in the United States over twenty years. Sivard, *World Expenditures*, 1987, 5. One of the U.S. tanks used in the war on Iraq only got one-half mile per gallon. It seems the U.S. needs oil to control oil.

39   "The United States of the World," *The Globe and Mail* (8 March 2003), F1.

40   The $75 billion military supplement is about $3,500 per Iraqi person. Imagine what this kind of expenditure could do to create the conditions for peace.

41   Michael Moore's Academy Award-winning documentary, "Bowling for Columbine," brilliantly explores violence in the United States in these terms.

42   Gordon Pitts, "Investors Spurred by War News," *The Globe and Mail* (22 March 2003), B4. There had already been a lot of profit-taking, even before the war, from fluctuating oil prices.

43   See Irwin Stelzer, "Bush Searches for Weapons of Mass Persuasion," *The Sunday Times* (16 February 2003). Under pressure for a Republican-controlled Congress, Bush Jr. finally had to agree to reduce his tax cut to $350 billion.

44   The Saskatchewan Chamber of Commerce spoke out against Premier Calvert's endorsing the no-war policy of the federal Liberals. But this was not to rally behind the American flag, but because this policy might hurt the chance of Saskatchewan firms getting post-war contracts in Iraq. You wonder if the American flag hasn't become a corporate logo.

45   These data are from Drew Fagan, "Working for the Yankee Dollar – not," *The Globe and Mail* (8 March 2003): F2.

46   For example, see Muray Dobbin, "Zip Locking North America: Can Canada Survive Continental Integration?" The Council of Canadians, no date. While this outlines the continued dangers of continentalism, the section on "foreign policy," clearly written

before the war on Iraq, paints a deterministic picture of Canada's subservience to the United States. In one place it states: "Canada will support U.S. positions no matter what…" (p. 31). Not quite. Clearly there is something fundamental missing in this analysis about Canada and emerging global politics in the face of Pax Americana.

47   See Wilhelm Reich, *The Mass Psychology of Fascism* (New York: Farrar, Straus and Giroux, 1946).

48   Elaine Monaghan, "US Fetes Its Mythical Heroine," *Herald Sun* (24 July 2003). It is daunting and frightening the extent to which militaristic and jingoistic propaganda is being created in the U.S. since the invasion of Iraq. By mid-summer, 2003, Canadians as well as Americans saw, displayed on their grocery-till newsstand, "How America Changed the world," (American Media Inc., 2003).

Bibliography

Ahmad, Eqbal, *Terrorism: Theirs and Ours*. New York: Seven Stories Press, 2001.

Barber, Benjamin R., *Jihad vs McWorld: How Globalism and Tribalism are Reshaping the World*. New York: Ballantine, 1996.

Blum, William, *Rogue State: A Guide to the World's Only Superpower*. Monro, Maine: Common Courage Press, 2000.

Harding, Jim, *After Iraq: War, Imperialism and Democracy*. Toronto: Fernwood, 2004.

Hourani, Albert, *A History of the Arab Peoples*. Cambridge, MA: Harvard University Press, 1991.

Kaplan, Robert D., *Warrior Politics: Why Leadership Demands a Pagan Ethos*. New York: Random House, 2002.

Knelman, F.H. *Reagan, God and the Bomb*. Toronto: McClelland and Stewart, 1985.

Reich, Wilhelm, *The Mass Psychology of Fascism*. New York: Farrar, Straus and Giroux, 1946.

Ritter, Scott, *War on Iraq*. Profile Books, 2002.

Salmi, Jamil, *Violence and Democratic Society: New Approaches to Human Rights*. London: Zed Books, 1993.

ACTING: PEACE ACTIVISM AND THE GLOBAL ANTI-WAR MOVEMENT

FINDING MY VOICE FOR PEACE

Dr. David Swann

Personal Background

My life was generally a pleasant adventure in a middle-class upbringing in Calgary, Alberta, in the latter half of the twentieth century, including six years of medical training. I had a vague sense that life was not like this for most of the planet. In spite of sympathy I could see little relationship then of those suffering in poor countries to my way of life. Travelling to South Africa in the late seventies to work in mission hospitals during apartheid changed my consciousness. Apart from the daily struggle to meet basic needs for most Africans, I discovered the price people paid to speak out against the white government. At the time Steve Biko, a courageous black activist, was killed in a jail cell near the Black homeland where I worked, with barely any media coverage. Speaking out is a costly matter and I was conscious, as never before, that I too would pay a price if I spoke out on discrimination in South Africa. I continued to do all I could medically, with a vague sense that, without political change, little would change in the health and opportunities for Black Africans.

Following my return to university to specialize in public health in the mid-1980s, my family and I went to the Philippines with a Primary Health Care project for one hundred communities. There I took the next step in understanding structural violence and the inequitable world order, in which I began to see Canada's part. As one Filipino peasant said in despair to me, "If I speak about the corruption I will be killed. If I don't speak about it, my family and I will starve!" This summed up the dilemma of life: telling the truth and not telling the truth can both be fatal where there is no justice and civil society. The stark desperation of life there and the appalling environmental decline left me profoundly depressed for many months after returning to Canada.

The 1991 Gulf War occurred soon after my return to Canada from the Phillipines, and I found my voice, both writing to political leaders and speaking locally for alternatives to the war. It was clear that Saddam Hussein's brutal regime had to be removed from their illegal occupation of Kuwait, but alternatives to war were never exhausted.

This led to my growing involvement in the anti-sanctions movement in the 1990s, against the decimation of Iraqi civil society, frequent bombing, and the destruction of basic infrastructure. In violation of the Geneva Convention and other international law, the water and sanitation damage contributed to appalling death rates, especially in the first few years. Conservative estimates from WHO and Red Cross place the death toll at over 750,000 children by 2002, due to malnutrition and lack of basic medical care, which had been part of an advanced health care system in Iraq until the 1991 war. Through the Canadian Network to End Sanctions on Iraq, we encouraged all citizens of conscience to speak against this misguided policy of economic and social deprivation in the name of containing a bad dictator.

From Kyoto to Baghdad

In October 2002, while employed by a regional health authority and, following ten years of public health work in rural
Alberta, I became increasingly involved and outspoken on
environmental and health issues including air quality and fossil fuel use, the health impact of intensive livestock operations,
tobacco control, and the national strategy for gun control. As
president of the Society of Alberta Medical Officers, I released
our position supporting the Kyoto Protocol as good policy for
health and the environment in Alberta. The Alberta environment minister was actively campaigning at the time against the
Kyoto Accord, and the chair of my health board was his con-
stituency president. I was fired within days of expressing this
position and, only following a national outcry was I invited to
return to employment there – an invitation I found to be dis-
ingenuous and rejected in favour of focusing more attention on
the crisis unfolding in Iraq. Even in Alberta I was discovering
the price of speaking out!

My dismissal galvanized my awareness of three key issues:
firstly, democracy is not free; secondly, the fossil fuel industry
(especially in Alberta) is a major political force; and thirdly,
powerful interests will go as far as possible to maintain control.
How far they will go depends on the balance of interests
such as independent media, other organized voices, and
political accountability. I had little time to reflect on these
philosophical and political realities at the time and, after
recovering emotionally, felt a sense of relief that I could now
get more involved in the worsening crisis unfolding in Iraq.

With public and media interest in me and in the
humanitarian issues in Iraq, I was able to communicate the
link between our dependence on oil in the western world (and
resistance to the Kyoto Accord) and U.S. vested interest in Iraqi

reserves, the second largest in the world. The link between government power, the oil-military interests, and media conglomerates in both countries was too obvious not to expose. It was clear to many of us that war would be terribly costly to the Iraqi population and risky for not only the Gulf region but for the future of Arab–Western relations in the future. From a health and humanitarian perspective I needed to communicate the profound risks to the Iraqi population of war and global stability if the United States violated international law and carried out a pre-emptive strike under the guise of protecting itself from terrorist attacks.

Iraq Mission: November 2002

Talk of war was well established in the fall of 2002, and it suddenly occurred to me that we were about to observe a terrible human catastrophe in Iraq from the security of our North American living rooms. The thought appalled me and I contacted Physicians for Global Survival (PGS) in Ottawa, the Canadian Red Cross, and a friend with Doctors Without Borders with two questions: what planning had been done to assist with this disaster in Iraq and was there an opportunity for me to go to Iraq, even at this late time, to assess medical preparedness and provide information to Canadians on what was needed?

PGS, a non-government organization committed to education for the prevention of war and elimination of nuclear arms use, responded positively to the idea, and I travelled to Iraq between 16 November and 16 December, 2002, via Amman, Jordan. Travelling with me was an Iranian Canadian, Dr. Amir Khadir, with Médecins du Monde, from Montreal, with similar goals. Our independent reports were produced within weeks of returning and circulated to colleagues, activists, and politicians across Canada in hopes of strengthening the budding anti-war movement. In my report I tried to sketch briefly a picture of the very hard life of people in Iraq under the most brutal sanctions in history. These sanctions followed two decades of relative abundance and development as a result of their oil wealth, including inexpensive food, cheap transportation, and free, modern health care and education for all. Clearly the contrast for Iraqi citizens was painful indeed, and most blamed the U.S. Administration and its influence at the UN for this decade of suffering – not Saddam Hussein.

In Baghdad I met a retired engineer who spoke of the prospect of war in this way: "First you tell me I have a headache, and then, to relieve me, you decide to chop off my head!" Given the carnage of the war that ensued, these comments return to haunt many of us. I met only a single individual who believed war was the best solution to the problems of terrorism or the oppression of Iraqis. No one is disappointed at the overthrow of Saddam Hussein, but the cost both to the country and to international institutions, including the UN, has been great.

Dr. Khadir and I experienced an extraordinary cooperation and assistance by Iraqi officials in meeting with individuals and humanitarian organizations we chose. Some of the mortality statistics were disturbing indeed and, while produced by credible organizations, such as UNICEF, could not be verified from primary sources.

We reviewed government data and reports from UN agencies (United Nations Development Programme, UNICEF, and WHO), non-governmental organizations, and committee meetings. In addition there were numerous interviews with International Red Cross, CARE, Médecins du Monde, Enfants du Monde, Première Urgence, and Architects for People in Need relating to disaster preparedness in Iraq as well as with many citizens and health workers, including physicians and nurses in Baghdad, Basra, and Mosul.

Our Findings

Since Iraq was seriously cut off from the world, the sanctions stifled human development at all ages and in every walk of life. The Oil-for-Food program, started six years after the end of the Gulf War and managed by the UN, provided the minimum of basic foodstuffs and medicines for survival. The psychological toll was evident in all our interactions and surely contributed to massive increases in medical demands.

Individuals and families we met were remarkably helpful and accepting of our mission and gave an important human dimension to the study. One family – that of Karima in central Baghdad – had particular challenges even without the war. This widow of eight years coped with great courage with her nine children in a two-room dwelling, selling condiments on the street. Three of the teen children were also working to keep the family fed and could not attend school, despite a keen interest. Twin girls of twelve years playfully tried to teach me Arabic during my three visits to their home. They all survived on the monthly rations of the Oil-for-Food program – flour, rice, sugar, tea, lentils, oil, and a few vegetables. The father had been killed in his taxi when the brakes failed – a predictable consequence of economic sanctions.

Hard Facts

The physical environment in Iraq (air, water quality and sanitation, vehicle and building safety) was poor and placed extra risk on all, but especially on the most disadvantaged. The United Nations Development Programme (UNDP 2002) reported 60 per cent access to safe drinking water, but this assumes a functional pumping system with consistent electricity, which is not the case. Garbage is seen everywhere

– streets, parks, empty lots, and playgrounds – attracting rats, packs of wild dogs, and poor people, young and old. Public service was extremely limited due to lack of trucks and cash to pay employees. Vehicles were abysmally maintained, except for those of the wealthy. Taxis were missing door handles and even lights. Even with marginal braking systems, they travelled at high speeds and polluted terribly. Roads were not maintained well during the sanctions, and, especially outside Baghdad, multiple hazards existed. Vehicle-related injury was commonplace, as would be expected, and there was minimal evidence of traffic control.

The economic conditions for over half of the population were desperate and caused widespread anxiety and stress, particularly when unexpected expenses arose such as home maintenance and health problems. With the sanctions since 1990, the dinar, formerly equivalent to US$3, was devalued by over six-thousand-fold, forcing people to sell personal possessions to survive. Many people, especially young people, gave up school or career in order to feed their families. Some of the monthly food rations were sold in order to meet such pressing needs. According to the UN many aspects of the food program were functioning with 94 per cent of funds for food, housing, and oil spare parts being available to those in need. Other sectors such as water, sanitation, education, electricity, agriculture, and health received substantially less of designated funds. The September 2002 UN Report on the Humanitarian Program indicated satisfactory distribution of commodities by the former Iraqi government, given the limitations in communications and transportation in Iraq at the time.

The entire health sector was profoundly degraded: lack of manpower and training, particularly in nursing; breakdown of infrastructure and inability to replace or repair equipment and acquire new technology; intermittent drug shortages; lack of transportation and weak communications. This contributed to many professionals leaving the country and meant an impoverished and demoralized workforce. Salaries (physicians earned twenty dollars a month and nurses are paid similarly) and working conditions discourage entry into the health professions. Patients had reduced access to care, incomplete investigations, and more expensive treatment options. Preventable conditions were common, due to a combination of marginal nutrition and poor water and sanitation. Diarrhoea, typhoid fever, hepatitis, influenza, and TB were common, with chronic conditions such as mental illness, heart disease and cancer increasing. International organizations, including Red Cross, CARE, and Première Urgence, assisted in some refurbishing of infrastructure in institutions, including water systems, but these remained unreliable due to power outages and drops in water pressure. Certain drugs (20% of essential drug lists) and much electronic and imaging technology were blocked from entry by the UN 661 Committee. Health status improved in some cases, especially in the northern Kurdish areas since the Oil-for-Food program began in 1996. Yet child health in particular remained precarious, with a shocking 24 per cent low birth weight (under 2,500 grams) and over 20 per cent malnutrition in children under five years.

Depleted uranium (DU) used in Gulf War armaments continues to be a plausible cause of the large increase in birth defects and childhood cancers reported by physicians in many hospitals, particularly in the Basra area. This has been noticed especially for leukemias and lymphomas, which appear also to be more aggressive and difficult to treat than in the past. The lack of any systematic review of increased incidence of cancers remains a matter of urgency and should be addressed in objective studies, especially in light of continued use of DU by the United States and other countries in their arsenal of conventional weapons.

Maternal mortality was another unacceptable result of the sanctions, with 294 deaths per 100,000 live births (three times higher than in 1990) due to maternal malnutrition, iron deficiency, unaffordable or inaccessible care, and inadequate emergency and health care services. Social problems increased in association with declining employment (43% for men; 10% for women) and falling literacy rates (from 90% in 1985 to 57% in 1997; UNDP 2002) as people focused on meeting basic needs. Sanctions included textbooks, computers, and all communications with the outside world, leaving teachers with low morale. Eighty-three per cent of schools were in disrepair, and over five thousand new schools are needed for the current population (UNDP 2002). Other problems included theft and increased numbers of street children, prostitution, and violence, which were rare prior to 1990.

Personal Observations

The people of Iraq touched me in many ways. Despite their suffering, they were cheerful and very hospitable – sharing the little they had with simplicity, humility, and dignity. Despite years of propaganda from their media against westerners, many Iraqis had a maturity and decency that recognized people as equal from our respective countries while seeing political leaders as responsible for problems in both our cultures. Their plea to us, on our returning to our home countries, was to put a human face on Iraqis. "We are not all Saddam Hussein or terrorists. You must stop treating us like insects," one woman exclaimed. Indeed.

Disaster Prevention: A Game Worth Trying

I argued, along with many organizations across the world and the United Nations, for active involvement in the critical work of preventing, as well as preparing for a U.S. invasion. Indeed the UN's purpose is to "protect future generations from the scourge of war," in part through its Charter which clearly identifies war as legal only where a country is being invaded (Article 51) or under the Security Council where no other option exists to restore peace to a country.

Disaster planning generally assumes the worst-case scenario and designs a strategy to mobilize human and material resources to minimize injury and death before disaster strikes. However, in the case of Iraq, we were dealing with a deliberate, manmade event (war). Among other factors, prevention hinged on a willingness to invest time, energy, and resources toward constructive resolution of conflict equal to that invested in preparations for war.

With weak medical and infrastructure support, extremely variable in each part of the country, extra demands of war meant dramatic loss of access to care for those with existing chronic disease as well as those in acute need during conflict.

Areas for Canadian Support to Iraq

Canada chose to stand with the UN and its Charter against the U.S. invasion, and many Canadians were very grateful for this sign of leadership, even statesmanship. As such Canada can continue to play a moderating role on the United States, foster civil society in Iraq and provide a reasoned voice for the legitimate role of the United Nations in peace-making and in rebuilding the country. The pressing need has become security, which is based on the lack of credibility and motives of the occupying U.S. forces. Financial and in-kind contributions through existing humanitarian organizations (e.g., International Committee of the Red Cross, MSF, Care International, and Doctors of the World) are critically needed. Faith-based organizations may also have a role to provide direct service to displaced persons, the ill, the injured, and the poor, but the danger is that evangelization could add enormously to the sense of violation of this Muslim land.

The Good News

The largest anti-war movement in human history arose as a result of this war. We know that in this the most violent of eras greater and greater armaments do not lead to greater security: witness the United States spending a billion dollars daily on military and weapons and a homeland security strategy that violates the rights and freedoms of U.S. citizens themselves. The real basis of human security lies in construction of better living conditions, equitable distribution of resources, and international trust. Constructive human and environmental development, unlike destructive war, would reduce rather than increase terrorism. In the post-war context we can see that the unilateral aggression by the United States:

- violated UN principles and process,
- destroyed lives on both sides of the conflict and increased refugees,
- provided no guarantee of better lives for Iraqis,
- risked nuclear and other weapons use,
- further destroyed the fragile environment,
- destabilized the Gulf region and may contribute to civil wars within Iraq,
- will contribute to extremism and terrorism,

- has major economic and social impacts on all countries and their citizens.

It is unfortunate that the U.S. Administration under George W. Bush does not appreciate the degree of violence done to Iraqis and other Arab citizens through its actions. The level of distrust and anger at the United States makes it impossible for it to be seen as a benevolent actor or liberator of Iraqis in this crisis. Other interests of the United States are also too evident – oil, strategic control in the Gulf, favoured relations with Israel, and others.

The UN, representing many countries, and limited as it is by its procedures, is still in the best position to balance individual state interests and preserve world order. It remains our best hope of avoiding arbitrary force by individual states and the endless cycles of violence we have witnessed. Our environments, economies, and social stability depend fundamentally on an international order grounded in law, as represented by the UN Charter and the Geneva and Hague Conventions.

The convergence of powerful political, military, and oil interests in the United States and in the United Kingdom, with compliant media, created an unprecedented momentum for war on Iraq. The rush to war, deliberate undermining of the role of the UN, and U.S. self-interest were revealed largely through the independent media and global Internet communications. The result was a second "super-power," an international community against the war that gave a powerful voice for an alternative vision for the planet.

Final Reflections

As a father, a citizen, and a physician, I have thought about what it means to be an ethical and responsible citizen of the world. I have been moved deeply by what I experienced of life in several countries, including apartheid South Africa, post-Marcos Philippines, and now Iraq, and realize the cost of silence. Democracy is only an idea until those of us able to speak and act freely do so. One elderly U.S. peace team member I met in Baghdad, Cynthia Banas, said this, when asked why she planned to stay there through the war: "It seems many people are willing to give their lives for war. More of us need to be willing to give our lives for peace."

For a large number of citizens on the planet, this conflict has awakened a consciousness that our very survival is dependent on recovering our vision for democracy, humanity, and the rule of law. We know there is a cost both to speaking and to remaining silent. The war in Iraq has touched us because it is ultimately about who we are, what we stand for in Canada, and what sacrifice we are willing to make to create a more sane and humane world for us and for our children.

References

Gordon, Joy. "Cool War – Economic Sanctions as a Weapon of Mass Destruction," *Harper's Magazine* (November 2002).

Kysia, Ramzi. *Malnutrition in Iraq: What the New UNICEF Study Shows* (22 November 2002); www.commondreams.org/views02.

Medical Action UK. *Collateral Damage: The Health and Environmental Costs of War on Iraq*, 12 November 2002, International Physicians for Prevention of Nuclear War; www.mapw.org.au/iraq/2002.

UNDP (United Nations Development Programme). Humanitarian Program in Iraq (September 2002); Living Conditions in Iraq

(September 2002); Country Brief for Iraq; and UN Representative Francis Dubois.

UNICEF. *The Situation of Children in Iraq* (UNICEF, 2002); www.casi.org.uk/info/unicef.

WHO Representative Office. *2001 Annual Report.*

Personal Communications

Ahmed Al-Hadithi, Dean, College of Veterinary Medicine.

Dr. A. Hallam, Uzzarah Cancer Hospital, Baghdad.

Dr. Baian Hassam, Pediatric Surgeon, Basra Maternity and Children's Hospital.

Dr. Mona Khomass, Dean, College of Science, Baghdad University.

Dr. Abduraman Suliyaman, Pediatric Surgeon, Mosul Jamhuri Pediatric Hospital.

Dr. Radh Tawalha, Medical Director, Iben Seena Hospital, Mosul.

Hennie Van Essen, Médecins du Monde Nursing Coordinator in Iraq, Baghdad Office.

FAITHFUL COUNTERPOINT TO WAR

Very Reverend Bill Phipps

A soldier deeply experienced in war once said: "I hate war as only a soldier who has lived it can; as one who has seen its brutality, its futility, and its stupidity."

The speaker was General Eisenhower, speaking in Ottawa in 1946. He also warned the world about the destructive, all-pervasive, and suffocating obscenity of the military- industrial complex. The integration of making instruments of war with products for domestic consumption pervades many American industries. General Electric is one example of a corporation with substantial defence contracts. Furthermore, few states of the union (perhaps none) are without companies with defence contracts. Elected officials do not want to jeopardize jobs dependent on the war machine.

It is unfortunate that the current commander-in-chief, i.e., president of the testosterone-laden United States administration, has had no personal, first-hand experience of war. He managed to avoid the Vietnam War, and not because of conscientious objection. The first nine months of the Bush administration were without vision, energy, or program. He had no compelling agenda. September 11th changed all that. Deeply influenced by his non-elected cabinet and other officials – Rumsfeld, Pearle, and Rice, for example, he found a clear, simple purpose, which was to make war on terrorists. With the new American agenda for the twenty-first century, the war on terrorism provided a popular cover to wage war on "America's enemies." When you are commander-in-chief of the world's most lethal war machine, it is easier to wage war than it is to build peace or attend to a complicated and troubling domestic agenda. And when you have an uncritical Congress, why bother with other divisive and complex issues?

There are three main reasons why the invasion and occupation of Iraq is wrong. First, war is outdated, passé, futile, and stupid. Ironically the destructive power of modern weapons renders them obsolete. Precision bombs are anything but. The cost in civilian life, environmental damage, and sheer dollars is prohibitive, and, except for the boys in power who seem to need their violence-fix, people around the world rebel at their deployment. Sanctions themselves led to at least 500,000 Iraqi deaths, most of them children. The civilian death toll of the actual four-week war is estimated to be a few thousand, but the wounded are in the tens of thousands. We will never know for sure. The depleted uranium poisoning land, soldiers, and civilians is a case in point.

Second, a massive use of force as carried out against Iraq can only lead to further anger and a more-determined commitment to acts of terrorism. Suicide bombers in Palestine and in Iraq itself are lining up to do damage to the enemy. The fear of suicide bombing being one of the few available weapons against the world's only superpower is very real. It is a new vehicle of guerrilla warfare. It will provide Bush and company with a never-ending threat to U.S. "security" and therefore perpetual war. It is beyond me how the heavy thinkers in Washington can ignore the inevitable violent backlash from a wider band of terrorists. Basic common sense, let alone human experience, knows that violence begets violence. When the United States pulls out of multi-lateral agreements and international actions, people see no alternative but to fight back with whatever tactics are available. When there is no hope in other solutions, what is there to lose?

Third, war is futile in our "globalized" world. The coordinated global peace campaigns, even before the U.S.-Iraq war started, were unprecedented. The United States may be a superpower militarily, but the countervailing global peace-builders expose the fundamental weakness and laziness of war as an instrument of foreign policy. Millions of people parading on the same day testify to a moral, common cause. A thousand performances worldwide of *Lysistrada* (the ancient Greek play whose women withdrew sex until their men withdrew from war) on the same day testify to humour as an instrument revealing war's futility. Global multi-faith peace vigils testify to the common religious traditions of non-violence. People who participate in multi-faith peace vigils do so for a variety of reasons. Public vigils declare their viewpoint about war and peace. Such events become personal testimonies to faith and public policy. They demonstrate solidarity with victims and fellow "vigilers" around the world. They embody hope in the human spirit and the Creator (however understood). And many people believe in the power of prayer (again, however understood). Lastly, peace vigils usually represent co-operative solidarity with other peace activism.

Global communication and solidarity instantly reveal the lies and manipulations of the propaganda from the powerful. Each of these ingredients of the new global conscience renders the purveyors of war impotent in their callous and hollow justifications. People question the goal of bringing "freedom" to Iraq when civil liberties are suspended in the United States. When the rationale for war constantly changes, people smell something foul. When no weapons of mass destruction are found, and no invasion of another country by Saddam Hussein occurs, "regime change" becomes the excuse for war. People begin to mistrust and become cynical. It doesn't help that some media become cheerleaders for Bush's war, abandoning their traditional critical function. Reliable language, as well as truth, becomes a casualty of war.

My observation after an extensive exposure tour of Israel and Palestine in January 2003 is that the two sides in that conflict can be characterized as those who are committed to peaceful solutions versus those who have no imagination and therefore rely on violence. There are outstanding people throughout both Palestinian and Israeli societies who could build a lasting peace if the minority war people would step aside. People in both societies are sick of being fearful and vulnerable. People in Israel and Palestine realize the futility of brute force. Their efforts are rarely reported in the media, whose idea of news is yet another suicide bomber in Tel Aviv or a tank rumbling through Hebron killing terrorists and civilians alike.

Then there is the financial cost in addition to the loss of life and ecological destruction. By any moral calculation, spending tens of billions of dollars (the U.S. invasion of Iraq will probably top $100 billion), killing thousands of people, desecrating the environment, and pummelling infrastructure in order to depose one man is obscene and immoral. Everyone knows that money spent to wage that one war would provide food, clean water, education, health care, and positive economic development for most of the developing world.

On a purely cost-benefit analysis, waging war instead of peace is immoral. The pure waste of the Earth's abundant, yet limited, resources is both unbelievable and unconscionable. How can anyone justify such expenditures? They can't. Recent U.S. foreign policy aside, there has been a relentless global movement toward international law, institutions, and treaties that recognize the futility of violence and promote positive interdependence of all life, including nation states. The International Criminal Court is only one example. It is unfortunate that the United States is withdrawing from these cooperative beacons of genuine hope. The best impulses of American society have much to contribute (as they have done in the past). I believe the bully mentality of the current administration may be the last gasp of weak men on steroids. The international community need not be bullied, bribed, nor beaten into submission to a fading ideology.

I believe the United Nations demonstrated great strength in January and February 2003 when it resisted U.S. intimidation. It took courage for nations who rely on U.S. aid, trade, and goodwill to say "No" to this immoral and illegal war. It was the United States that demonstrated weakness in not having the imagination, commitment, and intelligence to continue the international pathway in containing Saddam Hussein. It was the United States that abandoned the global community, not the other way around. To say Canada abandoned the United States in their time of need was absurd. On 11 September 2001, Canada was "there" for the United States. Just ask those Americans diverted to Newfoundland. Our government joined the United States in pouring billions of dollars into mutual "security." We joined the "war on terror" against Afghanistan, recommitting troops as the war on Iraq commenced. However, Canada believes in the United Nations and believes, along with most of the world, that increased support of the UN is the best way to peace with justice. By the way, where was the United States in 1939, 1940, and 1941 when Hitler *had* overrun Europe and thousands of Canadians were dying for freedom? They were nowhere, Mr. President.

Through hundreds of global organizations and twenty-first century means of communication, I believe that we are beginning the age of true internationalism. Even the overwhelming power of the United States will not be able to stem the tide of the irresistible global movement of peace with justice. My work on behalf of peace is centred on my role as an international president of the World Conference on Religion for Peace (WCRP). Founded in 1970, WCRP is an international peace organization representing the major religious traditions of the world. Active in over forty countries, WCRP supports local communities in building interfaith actions for peace. They have been active in creating a climate for reconciliation and peace in such places as Sierra Leone, Bosnia, and Kosovo. In its seventh world assembly in Amman, Jordan, WCRP declared:

> *The common ethical concerns embodied in all religious traditions call us to be individually and socially responsible for our neighbours and those in need. They help us draw on the sources of love, duty and responsibility as the foundations that undergird the establishment of justice.*

This global multi-faith organization sponsors work concerning AIDS, peace education, disarmament and security, conflict transformation, justice for children, and a global network of religious women's organizations.

Regardless of theology or doctrine, most religious traditions of the world share a common social ethic. Love of neighbour, peace with justice, harmony with Creation, mutual respect, dignity, and wholeness are ingredients in the ethical framework of the world's faiths. Increasingly the elements we share are greater than our disagreements. I believe that it is time for the mainstream "liberal" expressions of religious faith to step forward as representing the integrating and cooperative spirit of religion in contrast to the divisive "fundamentalist" minority.

No one has a corner on "the truth." One exciting aspect of living in an age of global communication is discovering the rich experience and traditions of so many expressions of faith. To learn the myths that motivate reverence and compassion; to realize the commonalties of ancient and eternal stories that define who we are; to share the beauty, texture, and vitality of each other's "holy" walk is not only inspiring; it is the future. No war machine nor oppressive ideology will be able to stop this journey into genuine global respect and partnership.

Canada is a place and space where discovering how to live together with all the world cultures is possible. Wherever I have travelled (Africa, Middle East, Central America, Asia), people still express hope and confidence in Canada's vocation as peace-builders. If we don't blow it, we are still trusted. I believe our national identity for the twenty-first century can be one of helping create "cultures of peace."

Our multicultural cities, our strong commitment to the United Nations, our overall foreign policy can lead the way in showing the world that peace with justice is possible. With a growing global jurisprudence, global institutions, and commitment to global cooperation gaining strength and credence, the way of the bully will become the way of the past. Fostered by the gutsy strength of the UN, we witnessed an unprecedented discussion of the legalities and morality of war before the United States invaded Iraq. The world's so-called superpower was forced to act unilaterally in their immoral and illegal aggression. Their defiance of international solidarity was transparent for all to see.

The world still needs to develop effective means to curtail and to control the killing madness of a Saddam Hussein. I believe it is possible. The International Criminal Court is just beginning its work. There's no reason why an effective UN "police force" cannot be developed. The key, however, is the continuing movement of civil society around the world. Closing the gap between rich and poor, creating a culture of peace within which children are raised, respecting indigenous cultures, honouring the integrity of Creation, and building bridges of international solidarity are some of the building blocks toward peace with justice. Continuing these efforts will render war obsolete.

Peace must be seen in its fullest sense. Peace is possible when the grievances concerning poverty, racism, sexism, disease, and oppression of all kinds are addressed honestly, openly, effectively, and with compassion. When the people of the world embrace one another in common cause, it will be inevitable that "the nations shall learn war no more" (Isaiah 2: 4).

PEACE ACTIVISM: A CANADIAN'S INVOLVEMENT IN THE IRAQ CONFLICT

Donn Lovett

"One drop in the ocean, but each drop can swell the tide" – Judy Small

It was fall, 1962. I was thirteen years old and the world was on the brink of a nuclear war. This time the given reason was the deployment of missiles in Cuba by the Russians. Something, apparently, the United States disagreed with. I remember those days as if they occurred last week. I spent six months of my life in constant stress. If I slept, I had nightmares about nuclear war. While awake I constantly thought of nuclear war and the destruction that would result, including my death. I remember the federal Canadian government organization called the Emergency Measures Organization (EMO), telling me that in the event of a nuclear attack while I was at school, I should hide under my desk. Remember, I was thirteen and, even at that age, I knew that "under the desk" was where they would find the vapour from the nuclear explosion – provided, of course, there was someone around to look for the vapour.

I remember one particular Monday evening. I know it was Monday because I delivered the *Star Weekly* magazine on that day. It was September in Winnipeg and after 6:00 p.m. when the sun was setting and the street was getting dark. Suddenly the air was filled with the unprecedented sound of air raid sirens. I panicked and, running to the first house I could find, I pounded on the door. The man who met me immediately recognized my problem, tried to answer my stream of questions quickly and attempted to calm me. He put me in front of his television to show me that the sirens were part of what the EMO referred to as a "mock nuclear attack," and I should not be afraid. How dare my government do this to a thirteen-year-old child? They staged a "mock nuclear attack," sounding air raid sirens without warning. I knew I had to do something to prevent a complete personal collapse. I sought people with whom I could discuss these issues and who were already doing something about the proliferation of nuclear weapons. I joined a peace movement and learned what "one person can do."

Also, vivid in my memory was the fact that the Cuban Missile Crisis was solved, not because one country attacked another, but rather as an outcome of dialogue. Yes, the Russians sent ships and the Americans countered with more ships, but ultimately dialogue prevented a war and the United Nations was involved in the solution. This message that I received from the events of 1962 still resonates today. That is, that dialogue is still the best way to solve disputes and the United Nations Organization is needed more than ever.

My activism carried me through high school and the Vietnam War. The point is my activism was born out of these events and the tumultuous sixties. In 1981 I found myself living in Baghdad and working for a Canadian company called Canron. We were providing water pipe and fittings to Iraq for the supply of drinking water. The Iraqi regime had decreed that everyone in Iraq would have clean drinking water and properly treated sewage. As a Canadian company, we were doing millions of dollars of trade in Iraq, and I was sent to administer the contracts. My experience living among the people of Iraq and interacting with them was one of respect, kindness, and honesty. When the Gulf War broke out and the United States talked about collateral damage for the first time, I thought of my Iraqi friends, and so I saw the war from a different perspective than did most North Americans.

I followed the events in Iraq and learned about the effect of the embargo on the people of Iraq and in particular the increased infant mortality. My daughter was born in December 1990 and, being a stay-at-home father, I was deeply involved in raising my child, and I readily empathized with those Iraqis who were losing their children at an alarming rate. Reports of the rise in infant mortality and deaths of civilians were stalled by the United States and the United Kingdom at the UN. They blocked reports coming from the World Health Organization and UNICEF. Finally, the information could no longer be hidden, and the Oil-for-Food program was initiated in an attempt to alleviate the hunger to which years of embargo had subjected the Iraqi people.

We learned that during the 1991 Gulf War, the United States led bombing raids that attacked every hospital, every water treatment plant, every wastewater plant, most schools, and every major intersection in downtown Baghdad in order to destroy the water distribution and sewage collection systems. All attacks against civilian infrastructure are in direct violation of the UN Charter and must be considered war crimes. A good friend of mine, Denis Halliday, the former UN Humanitarian Coordinator in Iraq said: "We are in the process of destroying an entire society. It is as simple and terrifying as that. It is illegal and immoral." Pre-1990 Iraq reflected the status of a modern developing society, in which the wealth it obtained from exporting its main commodity, oil, contributed to improving the quality of life of the Iraqi people. The Government of Iraq made sizable investments in the education sector from the mid-1970s until 1990. Educational policy included provision for scholarships, research facilities and medical support for students. By 1989 the combined primary and secondary enrolment stood at 75% (slightly above the average for all developing countries at 70%). Illiteracy had been reduced to 20% by 1987. Education accounted for over 5% of the state budget, which was superior to the average for developing countries at 3.8%.

After the imposition of sanctions in 1991, we know that:

1. 1.5 million Iraqi civilians have died since 1991 as a direct result of the sanctions.

2. 600,000 of the dead were children under 5 years of age according to UNICEF reports and substantiated by the Red Cross. A recent UN report stated that the infant mortality rate in Iraq is 133. This means that for every 1,000 children born, 133 will not reach the age of five. By comparison, Canada's infant mortality rate is less than four.

3. The number of malnourished children has increased over 300% since 1991.

4. Maternal mortality rates have more than doubled during this period of the sanctions and 70% of Iraqi women suffer from anemia.

5. Unemployment has soared under the sanctions, as has inflation. The average civilian salary, for example, is C$3.60 per month.

6. An estimated 800 tonnes of depleted uranium contained in ammunitions were used by the allied forces in the Gulf War. Cancer rates in Iraq have increased five-fold since the Gulf War. Childhood leukemia in Iraq has the highest rate in the world.

These undeniable facts lead me to travel to Iraq to view first hand the devastation to the Iraqi civilian population and the complete destruction of the civilian infrastructure and the civilian economy. I could no longer stand by and let the crimes continue, crimes to which the Canadian government was a partner. Tacit approval of the unjust conditions to which Iraqis were subjected was tantamount to direct involvement in the destruction.

I began to contact people I thought could give me information to help me develop a plan of action to assist the people of Iraq. The first was Denis Halliday. I remembered reading a statement that Mr. Halliday had made after he resigned his position with the UN in protest over U.S. interference in the relief operations in Iraq. He said, "I can find no legitimate justification for sustaining economic sanctions under these circumstances. To do so in my view is to disregard the high principles of the United Nation's Charter, the Convention of Human Rights, the very moral leadership and the credibility of the United Nations itself."

Secretary-General Kofi Annan appointed Denis J. Halliday, an Irish national, to the post of United Nations Humanitarian Coordinator in Iraq, at the Assistant Secretary-General level on 1 September 1997. Halliday served as such until the end of September 1998. During this period, the Security Council Resolution 986 Oil-for-Food Program, introduced in 1996/97 to assist the people of Iraq under the economic sanctions imposed and sustained by the Security Council, was more than doubled in terms of oil revenues allowed. This enabled the introduction of a multi-sectored approach, albeit modest, to the problems of resolving malnutrition and child mortality. Mr. Halliday resigned from the post in Iraq, and from the United Nations as a whole, on 31 October 1998, after serving the organization for thirty-four years.

After running the Oil-for-Food program, which uses Iraqi oil revenues to distribute basic food rations and medical aid to Iraqi civilians, Halliday turned his attention to spreading the word about sanctions-related suffering. I contacted Mr. Halliday in late 1999 and invited him to Canada. We met in

Ottawa for a series of lectures, and I took him to the House of Commons to meet the then Chair of the Standing Committee on Foreign Affairs, Mr. Bill Graham. I wanted him to ask Mr. Graham to hold hearings on Iraq at the Standing Committee. Graham agreed immediately and the hearing was scheduled for March 2000. I arranged for Mr. Halliday and Mr. Arthur Millholland, the president of Oilexco, the only Canadian company participating in the Oil-for-Food program, to come to Ottawa as witnesses to the committee. The hearings lasted for three days, culminating in Report #5, "Resolution on Iraq," which was tabled in the Canadian House of Commons on 12 April 2000.

Report #5, which was unanimously supported by the eighteen members of Parliament sitting on the committee and representing all five political parties, called for a de-linking of sanctions. This meant the removal of economic sanctions but leaving military sanctions in place. It further called for an opening of dialogue between Canada and Iraq. The deputy prime minister of Iraq, Mr. Tariq Aziz, accepted Report #5 as a good basis to resolve the situation in Iraq. It was suggested that the secretary-general of the United Nations might use this report as a basis for breaking the impasse on getting proper humanitarian relief to Iraq.

Report #5 was rejected outright by the then Canadian foreign minister, Lloyd Axworthy, and it died without being taken to the UN. The main reason given by senior advisors to Axworthy, at a meeting that I attended, were as follows: "While we recognize the destruction to the people of Iraq, we cannot do anything to upset the U.S. Administration because they will beat us up on trade." One of the senior advisors was a medical doctor who had visited Iraq and had seen first hand the difficulties being experienced by the people of Iraq.

This resulted in two important outcomes for me. I met Madame Colleen Beaumier, the vice-chair of the Standing

Committee on Foreign Affairs, and I discovered that Lloyd Axworthy would not act if it meant confronting the United States.

I invited Madame Beaumier to come to New York to meet with the deputy prime minister of Iraq, Mr. Tariq Aziz. She agreed and the meeting was arranged for September 2000 at the Iraq Permanent Mission to the UN in New York. We discussed Report #5 as a basis to solving the economic embargo on Iraq while agreeing that at this stage the military embargo had to remain in place. The meeting was cordial and it was the first time that parliamentarians from Canada and Iraq had met since the Gulf War. By now Canada had closed its embassy in Baghdad, even though Iraq maintained a *chargé d'affaires* in Ottawa. The action now became one of getting individual MPs to endorse Report #5 in an attempt to get a majority of the 301 MPs to sign a letter addressed to the prime minister (and copied to the foreign minister) demanding that Canada accept the results of the report drafted by the Standing Committee. We received unanimous support from the Bloc Québécois, the New Democratic Party, and the Progressive Conservatives, while individual members of both the Liberal Party and the Alliance Party, led by Dr. Keith Martin, agreed to endorse the report. We had the support of 127 members when Parliament was dissolved on 22 October 2000, and an election called. This nullified our efforts until after the election.

A new parliament was elected in November 2000, and we restarted our efforts to get Report #5 accepted by the Canadian Government. However, we now faced a new resistance. John Manley was appointed to the position of foreign minister, and he took an even closer stance with Washington. During Manley's tenure, Canada moved as close to Washington as Canada had ever been. This caused individual MPs in the Liberal ranks to distance themselves from any initiative that may confront the United States. We also witnessed a hardening of a pro-U.S. position with the Alliance Party, under their new leader, Stockwell Day. Although we still held the support of the Bloc, the NDP and the Tories, getting majority support was becoming increasingly more difficult. This, combined with the election of the neo-conservative Bush administration, made the matter of getting a resolution of the Iraqi sanctions almost impossible. It became clear to me that removal of sanctions could not happen without the return of the weapons inspectors and a resolution on the question of Weapons of Mass Destruction (WMDs), which became the buzzword of the Bush White House.

At this time the Bush White House had little or no interest in foreign relations. It seemed hunkered down in an isolationist mentality until the attack on the World Trade Center in September 2001. The ensuing "War on Terrorism" set a course for Bush and his neo-conservative cohorts that continue to affect the world in a seriously negative way. The appetite for war, demonstrated by Bush after the September attack, provoked me to call a meeting of international diplomats and interested individuals to meet in New York to see what we could do to dampen the U.S. enthusiasm for war. I contacted Denis Halliday and Hans von Sponeck, both former United Nations humanitarian coordinators in Iraq. I contacted Scott Ritter, the former U.S. marine major and head of the UN weapons inspections in Iraq from 1991 through 1998. I also asked the former foreign minister of Canada, Lloyd Axworthy, to join us, along with the president of the Canadian oil company, Oilexco, Arthur Millholland. Lloyd Axworthy had had a change of heart since leaving Ottawa and wanted to see what could be done to ease the pressure on Iraqi civilians. All agreed and a meeting was arranged for the end of November 2001 in New York, ironically held at the Republican Women's Center. Mr. von Sponeck could not join us but was in contact via phone and e-mail.

Although several ideas were discussed, it became clear that the return of the weapons inspectors was the only way out of the impasse. It was thought that Canada could play a role, given that it had an outstanding reputation at the UN and was not an imperialist nation. Iraq might accept recommendations coming from there. However, John Manley was still foreign minister in Canada and not predisposed to anything that may confront the United States. We decided to continue discussions and to formulate a plan that could be discussed between Canada, Iraq, and the UN.

Lloyd Axworthy agreed to discuss our meeting with Louise Frechette, a Canadian and the deputy secretary-general of the UN, and with Colin Powell, the U.S. secretary of state, whom he was to meet with at dinner while he was in New York and Washington. Conversations within the group continued over the last part of 2001 and into 2002.

In January 2002, Prime Minister Chrétien appointed Bill Graham as the new Canadian foreign minister, and hopes for a more sovereign Canadian position with regard to the United States gave us a reason to quicken our attempts to get the weapons inspectors back into Iraq. By this time Denis Halliday and Hans von Sponeck were now concentrating their efforts in Europe. Arthur Millholland was in the UK and busy with his business efforts. Lloyd Axworthy became busy with his UBC institute. It was left to Scott Ritter and me to continue the discussions started in New York in the fall of 2001.

Scott Ritter arranged to meet with the Labour Party in the UK and the French Government to discuss the return of the inspectors. I began to build support in Ottawa with MPs with whom we could work. Notably, Madame Francine Lalonde of the Bloc, Dr. Keith Martin of the Alliance, Joe Clark of the Conservatives, and Alexa McDonough of the NDP were contacted, and they agreed to keep in touch with the initiative. Madame Lalonde became quite active and was a strong source of support. I was in constant contact with Madame Colleen Beaumier, who gave us access to the Liberal caucus.

Meanwhile, I developed a relationship with Robert Fry, the senior advisor to Bill Graham, the foreign minister, as well as with Chris Hull and Graeme McIntyre from the Department of Foreign Affairs and International Trade (DFAIT). Through Robert Fry we could get access to the foreign minister if the matter was significant enough. At this point we were feeling quite encouraged and I asked the Standing Committee to meet with Scott Ritter to discuss the return of weapons inspectors. Thanks to the efforts of Madame Lalonde and Dr. Martin, the committee agreed to meet with Scott Ritter and Denis Halliday in early June 2002.

The meeting with the Standing Committee was very successful. Scott Ritter was able to convey the importance of getting the weapons inspectors back into Iraq as a necessary step to getting the economic sanctions removed. There was a sense from the meeting that Canada could play a role once the inspectors had returned. Scott Ritter and I then met with Madame Lalonde to develop a document entitled "The Honest Broker." The thrust of this document was to ask Iraq to agree first to the return of the weapons' inspectors and then to permit Canada, South Africa, and Belgium to help mitigate any difficulties that might arise between Iraq and the UN as a consequence of the inspections. These countries would not interfere with the inspectors themselves because they recognized that the United States would not tolerate any interference with the inspection process. However, situations might have arisen requiring some form of reconciliation between the UN and Iraq during the inspections. Canada was chosen because it is the major trading partner of the United States with a close historical, political, and geographical relationship. South Africa was chosen to represent the non-aligned nations and Belgium because of its membership in NATO and the EU.

In August 2002, Scott Ritter went to South Africa to meet with the Tariq Aziz of Iraq, Mr. Pahad, the deputy foreign minister of South Africa, and the Belgian foreign minister. During these meetings it was agreed that Scott would go to Baghdad to address the Iraq National Assembly on 8 September and during the presentation would discuss the return of the inspectors. South Africa and Belgium agreed to cooperate with Canada, if Canada would take the lead on the "honest broker" initiative.

Meanwhile back in Canada, I stayed in touch with the prime minister and the foreign minister to ensure that, at the very least, Canada would continue to support the UN and not support U.S. unilateral actions. On two occasions in July and August of 2002, in direct phone conversations with Prime Minister Chrétien, I was assured that Canada would keep supporting the UN. On 9 August 2002, at a meeting with Bush in Detroit, Mr. Chrétien reiterated Canada's support for a UN resolution to the Iraq situation. At the same time I had met with Minister Graham, who also assured me that Canada would stay with a UN resolution. They have maintained that position, and I believe that Canadians should be very proud of their actions in the face of the tremendous pressure from the United States. I was in the Canadian House of Commons on 17 March 2003, when the prime minister announced that Canada would not support the U.S. war on Iraq. This was one of the bravest things he had ever done.

Scott Ritter met with the Iraq National Assembly on 8 September 2002, and told them in no uncertain words that they had to allow the inspectors to return and that there was no room for negotiations on this matter. Further, they had to advise the UN that they would accept the inspectors before the United States was able to get a resolution before the UN that they would not be able to deal with. Iraq accepted what Scott Ritter had to say and dispatched Foreign Minister Sabri to New York for 14 September.

While this was being organized and unfolding, Bush was dragged kicking and screaming to the UN on 12 September. This happened through the efforts of a number of countries including Canada and the United Kingdom. He appeared at the UN because there was virtually no support for U.S. actions against Iraq and Bush felt that the United States could beat the UN into submission. The timing worked out for Iraq, which had agreed to come to New York for 14 September and, through a series of negotiations in New York that I was involved in, made its proposal to the UN through Kofi Annan on 16 September 2002. The proposal allowed for a return of weapons inspectors to Iraq with no conditions attached. The negotiations were finalized in November 2002 and the way was paved for Hans Blix to return to Iraq after four years without inspections.

The return of the inspectors neutralized the U.S. demand that Iraq disarm. However, it soon became apparent that the United States was not interested in a disarmed Iraq but rather wanted control of the country for several reasons, not the least of which was Iraqi oil and the fact that in their war on terrorism they had not been able to find Osama bin Laden. The United States then moved to the language of "regime change," and the world began to respond to their actions, culminating in the mass rallies held worldwide on 15 February 2003. Tens of millions of people protested the U.S. position, including 1.5 million people in London, who opposed Tony Blair's pro-U.S. stance, and one million people in Rome, who opposed their government's support for the United States. Spain saw hundreds of thousands of people in Madrid and Barcelona protesting the Spanish government's support of Bush. As a result, the United States changed its rhetoric from "regime change" to "liberation of the Iraqi people and a change in human rights."

In January 2003 I organized a parliamentary delegation to go to Iraq with the knowledge of both the prime minister and the foreign minister. Madame Colleen Beaumier and her able assistant, Natalie Jewett, joined me on the trip. In Baghdad we met with the deputy prime minister, Mr. Tariq Aziz, the foreign minister, Mr. Naji Sabri, the Iraq trade minister, the communications and transportation minister, the deputy agriculture minister, and the deputy speaker of the Iraq National Assembly, accompanied by several members of the Assembly. The purpose of the trip was to convey to Iraq the Canadian position with regard to disarmament and to receive any message that Iraq wanted put before our government. The Iraqis asked one thing and that was for Canada to maintain its position in support of the UN.

We arrived back in Canada on 29 January 2003, and worked non-stop to try and reach agreement on an initiative that would prevent the United States from invading. This involved a two-stage proposal. Initially there was the six points for peace plan that was developed through the efforts of Scott Ritter and the deputy foreign minister of South Africa, Mr. Pahad, and was an extension of the Canadian initiative that was being discussed by the non-permanent members of the UN Security Council in February 2003. After the attack by the United States and the United Kingdom, a modification of that plan which was now being sponsored by the Vatican was tabled. Both of these proposals had been somewhat agreed to by Iraq and involved disarmament, human rights, democracy, diplomacy, economy, and, of course, peace. But as the entire world now understands, the United States and the United Kingdom were not interested in a peaceful solution to Iraq.

The point of this article is to let people know that anyone can make a difference. Although we failed in our attempt to prevent the United States from invading Iraq, we accomplished great things during the past few years. Canada did not change its position and support the U.S./UK war. Canada maintained its support for the UN. We met with several governments around the world and we felt we influenced their decisions. Often it is very ordinary Canadians who make a difference. For example, my twenty-three-year-old daughter, Shanda, travelled to Iraq in 1999 as part of an international women's conference. While in Iraq she visited several schools and talked to children about the sanctions. She was invited to meet with Madame Aline Chrétien and in December 1999 had a ninety-minute audience with Madame Chrétien to discuss her experience in Iraq. Shanda and her younger sister Kate have become anti-war activists in there own right. The unwavering support of my wife Nora has been crucial to both our daughters' and my activism.

Our responsibility now is to ensure that the United States does not become the judge, jury, and executioner for the world. We shall overcome.

Epilogue: September 2003

A large group of activists and academics travelled to Cyprus in April 2003 to discuss what to do next. Out of those discussions came the dream of Dr. Tareq Ismael of the University of Calgary to build an International University in Baghdad (IUB). The initial proposal was developed in Cyprus, and it was decided that the initiative should be a Canadian-sponsored one.

The IUB would begin as a "virtual university," meaning that the project will begin to get underway in terms of establishing programs, international connections, and so forth, even before it would acquire a physical presence in Iraq. Once established, however, it will be a graduate-focused institution and would complement post-secondary education in Iraq, rather than compete in the post-Baath environment. Not only will the university spearhead needed educational programs, but it will also make available a wealth of educated individuals capable of filling the "brain-drain" that resulted from the years of war, militarization, and sanctions. Before the U.S. and British-led attack on Iraq, there were ten universities in the country, but the quality of education provided at these universities was in decline as there was not enough funding available to run these institutions properly, principally due to the UN Security Council sanctions and the choices made by the previous Iraqi government to focus predominantly on militarization. Vast numbers of university professors and professionals, such as doctors and engineers, left the country in the 1990s as a result of the dramatic decline in social services. Now, largely due to the destruction and looting incurred in the recent war and its aftermath, none of the universities in Iraq remain fully functional. This is a predicament that urgently requires attention, as access to education has always been instrumental in developing a lively and independent civil environment.

The established universities in Iraq will benefit greatly from an internationally oriented, graduate studies facility in their country. The IUB will be able to draw students from all over the world to study in Iraq, alongside Iraqi citizens, creating a constructive dialogue that is capable of transcending the simplicities of international conflict scenarios. The breadth of experiences possessed by the international students will enhance the resources and connections that Iraqi citizens themselves would have, fostering greater civil society through an ever-increasing independence from governmental contacts. At the same time, the unique experiences of the Iraqi students – historically, politically, economically, and culturally – along with the potential revival of a "cosmopolitan" Baghdad, will serve to enrich the international students who would be studying at the IUB.

The planning committee has already garnered a great deal of international recognition for this project, including support from individuals such as Betty Williams, the Irish Nobel laureate, and Jordan's Prince el-Hassan Bin Talal, brother of the late King Hussein, who is acting as the chairman of the board of trustees. Furthermore, IUB advocates include Canada's former prime minister Jean Chrétien, along with Edward Broadbent, former leader of NDP; Richard Falk, professor of international law (emeritus) at Princeton University; and John Polanyi, winner of the Nobel Prize in chemistry and professor of chemistry at the University of Toronto. With the help of other supporters, the IUB planning committee is also currently working to urge Nelson Mandela, former South African president, to become a member of the university's board of trustees.

At this crucial time when many Iraqis see any outside involvement as largely negative and tied to an "occupation" and relate to the international environment in terms of "conflict," the reconstruction of Iraqi educational infrastructure through this project and others will help to provide an example for the positive possibilities of *international cooperation*. Canada is in a unique position to spearhead such a project and should seize the opportunity to foster positive development in Iraq and advance our traditional role as a peacemaker in the international environment.

Over the past few months, we have had meetings with several MPs, senators, DFAIT, CIDA and potential partner agencies such as the Association of Universities and Colleges of Canada, the Canadian Bureau for International Education, and the Social Sciences and Humanities Research Council of Canada. We presented them with the following rationale for why Canada should lead this initiative:

1. Canada has had a long-standing relationship with the Middle East and in particular with Iraq. Prior to the Gulf War of 1991, Canada was one of Iraq's primary trading partners, and the Canadian Wheat Board was the largest supplier of wheat to Iraq.
2. Canada is considered a non-imperialistic actor in the region. We have not had the expansionist policies of France, the United Kingdom and the United States.
3. Canada has had a reputation as a Middle Power and a peacemaker in world affairs.
4. The stance that Canada took in the recent Gulf War of not supporting unilateral U.S. action has reinforced Canada's image in world affairs.
5. Canada can exercise a tremendous amount of influence in Iraq and the region by taking these kinds of initiatives.

Anyone who finds this rationale compelling and is interested in helping us realize this project may contact me at donn@dlagency.com. This may be a small step for each of us, but for Iraqi society it is a major leap.

IRAQ, INTERNATIONAL LAW, AND RESPONSIBLE CITIZENSHIP

Dr. Arthur Clark

The United States and the United Kingdom invaded and occupied Iraq claiming that weapons of mass destruction (WMD) in Iraq represented a threat to international peace. To date no evidence to substantiate this claim has been found. But the invasion and occupation have demonstrated an unequivocal threat to international peace. By their unlawful use of force against the government of a sovereign state, the perpetrators – and particularly the government of the United States – have made unmistakable their potentially lethal threat to various governments worldwide, and therefore their threat to international peace. There is nothing subtle about this threat, and the "opinion leaders" in the Bush administration seem particularly eager to make the threat clear to anyone paying attention.

This threat did not begin with the Bush administration, and it is not unique to the government of the United States. Lawless violence, cloaked in noble intentions, is characteristic of powerful states. The United States, as the dominant power, is the current prototype. In our culture there is a general reluctance to recognize the threat we pose to others. Norman Cousins in his 1987 book, *The Pathology of Power* noted the tendency of power to create a language of its own, making other forms of communication suspect.[1] The United

States and the United Kingdom are unlikely to repudiate international law outright because they derive massive benefits from the international legal system. But their invasion of Iraq has destabilized the framework for international peace and security, produced thousands of casualties, devastated Iraqi cultural institutions, increased risks to Americans and others, and accelerated the drain of public resources into the military sector of the U.S. economy. Somebody, of course, has benefited handsomely from all this. But that is a topic for a different essay.

Calling for an investigation into the Bush administration's claims about Iraqi WMD has recently become politically acceptable, and even calls for impeachment are beginning to appear. It is not politically correct, however, to do anything that would fundamentally challenge the lawless violence of the government of the United States. Yet that challenge is essential to the future peace and security of North Americans. Any state or institution arrogating to itself the right to threaten others will thereby jeopardize its own security. The costs of maintaining that security will increase, draining public revenues and devastating the lives of individuals. It is unrealistic to think that security for North Americans can be reliably promoted without promoting the security of others. But conventional wisdom accepts the preposterous idea that our long-term security is being enhanced by escalating our threat to other countries. These issues, as elementary and urgent as they are, must be placed in the public arena by concerned citizens. Otherwise, they will not be taken seriously by political and intellectual "leaders."

From the Gulf War until the illegal invasion of Iraq in 2003, western policy toward Iraq was based on an intense and sustained hostility to the government of that country. This hostility has had devastating consequences for the people of Iraq. In North America, public support for this hostile policy has been cultivated using standard devices of war propaganda, notably demonization of the political leadership in the targeted country. Propaganda for war characteristically draws on factual information but removes it from context or places it in a context to evoke support for war. Outright lying is usually unnecessary.[2]

This essay provides some context for the themes which, removed from their context, have been used as propaganda for war against Iraq. It emphasizes the violations of international law by all parties to the conflict. It uses this background as an object lesson on the failure of responsible citizenship in our culture. I conclude with a proposal for a functional concept of responsible citizenship. Implementing that concept can improve the chances for peace and security in the future, not only for Iraq and other countries overseas, but for North Americans as well.

Invasion and Lawlessness

The standard North American view of Saddam Hussein's Baath government in Iraq has emphasized its treachery. Governments are often violent and deceitful, and the government of Iraq under Saddam Hussein has provided an important example. Much more telling examples are the five permanent members of the UN Security Council, since they have had, individually and in aggregate, a far more decisive influence on twentieth-century history than the government of Iraq. Each of those five countries has a history of murderous internal conflict and murderous and aggressive foreign policy.

This treachery of governments has historically been tolerated or supported by their citizens and by their allies. A standard way of achieving that toleration and support is the government's emphasis on the necessity of its own treachery to overcome an adversary's treachery. To the extent that this argument is effective, the problem will persist.

The case of Iraq illustrates this paradox. The invasion of Iraq by the United States and the United Kingdom was justified on the grounds that Iraq was a threat to the peace. It is irrational to support one government's armed attack on another based on the claim that the country being attacked might do something similar in the future. The invasion was also an assault on the principle of non-aggression, which is a necessary cornerstone of the international legal system. The invasion is illegal, and the argument in support of it is irrational.

Every major act of lawless violence opens a Pandora's box. The invasion and occupation of Iraq were expected to increase recruitment into terrorist organizations and emerging evidence supports the prediction. The U.S./UK aggression will prompt a range of countermeasures from governments around the world. We cannot predict these developments in detail, but the dangers may have massively increased. The larger problem of lawless violence has been made worse by using lawless violence against the government of Iraq.

A powerful state can often persuade the public to abandon reason and common sense in support of its violence and treachery. Because every powerful state also facilitates major positive achievements and conveys important benefits, the grateful public is easily seduced into support for the state's villainy. An act of military aggression by a powerful state will reflect this ambivalent nature. An act of aggression produces irreparable harm and major atrocities. Part of the irreparable harm will be the increased volatility and a waste of resources that attend lawless violence. But the act of aggression will also be associated with ample benefits and positive effects. And the propagandist can use that aspect of reality to recruit support for further acts of lawless violence.

Iraq's Brutal Dictatorship

The rise of Saddam Hussein's murderous dictatorship can be understood in much the same way. It was probably perceived by its supporters as a necessary evil in defence against mortal dangers. In Iran (1953), Guatemala (1954), and Chile (1973), more open governments had been overthrown with the assistance of the U.S. Central Intelligence Agency. The CIA had also helped the conspirators (including Saddam Hussein) who overthrew Iraq's popular revolutionary regime in 1963. Saddam's nationalist Baath party was therefore keenly aware of the danger of internal subversion, and particularly one directed from Washington. Thus the danger of subversion was used to justify the savage internal security apparatus set up by Saddam Hussein. The measure was temporarily successful on its own terms. The CIA never did to the Baath in Iraq what they had done in Iran, Guatemala, and Chile.

Iraq's Brutal Repression of the Kurds

The Baath government had also carried out murderous attacks against the armed Kurdish insurgency in northern Iraq, and villages known to support it. Like so many other acts of the Iraqi government, these attacks were astonishing in their brutality. They exceeded even the Turkish attacks on Kurdish insurgents and villages in that country and rivalled the attacks by Guatemalan armed forces on Guatemalan villages after 1954. This is state terrorism, the form of terror that shaped the meaning of the word in the French Revolution of the late eighteenth century.

All these acts of violence occurred in a context that seemed, to some observers, to justify the atrocities. The Iraqi government campaign was directed against Kurdish factions that had sustained an armed nationalist movement. An armed insurgency in a country surrounded by hostile states can reasonably be considered a "security threat."

There had been violent conflict between the Kurdish insurgents and the Iraqi government well before the Baath party came to power in Iraq. The Iraqi government, before and after the rise of Saddam Hussein, used a carrot-and-stick approach in dealing with the threat. In March 1970, an agreement had been worked out between the government in Baghdad and the Kurdish leadership, whereby Kurdish would be the official language of the region and any government official stationed there would have to speak Kurdish. There would be Kurdish representation in the central governing body of Iraq, and a Kurdish university would be established. By regional standards this was a remarkably progressive arrangement, and the accord, sponsored by the Iraqi government, was signed by the Kurdish leadership. But the Kurds continued to seek foreign support for their insurgency, the internal security threat to Iraq persisted, and with it the government's murderous repression.[3]

Iraq's Aggression

Iraq's major act of foreign aggression under Saddam Hussein was directed against Iran, beginning in 1980. It was ultimately responsible for hundreds of thousands of deaths and major setbacks to the economy in Iraq and in Iran.[4] Like Saddam Hussein's other acts of violence prior to 1990, the aggression against Iran was largely ignored or supported by other countries including the United States. That complicity changed suddenly in August 1990, when Iraq launched its aggression against Kuwait, a regional U.S. client ruled by a family dictatorship. Saddam Hussein's tyranny and aggression instantly became the subject of unrelenting propaganda for war in the western media.

The death toll resulting directly from Iraq's invasion and occupation of Kuwait is estimated at three to five thousand, higher than the death toll from the U.S. invasion of Panama a few months earlier, but lower than the death toll from Israel's invasion of Lebanon in 1982. Neither the U.S. invasion of Panama nor Israel's invasion of Lebanon became the object of effective action from the UN Security Council.[5] By contrast, in the case of Iraq, international law was applied, leading to a series of proposals from Iraq for a negotiated peaceful withdrawal from Kuwait.[6] Those proposals for a peaceful resolution of the crisis represent the intended effect of mechanisms established in the UN Charter.

But the UN Security Council had abdicated its decision-making authority to then president George Bush. Bush rejected Iraq's offers: "There will be no negotiations." By late December 1990, Iraq was seeking guarantees that their troops would not be attacked as they withdrew, that foreign armed forces in the region would go home after resolution of the crisis, that some steps toward resolution of the Palestinian problem would be made, and that some measure to control weapons of mass destruction in the Middle East would be initiated. The last point was a scarcely veiled reference to Israel's nuclear weapons program, which threatened Iraq.

The Iraqi offer was recognized as a "serious pre-negotiating position" by U.S. analysts. Instead of pursuing it, as would be required under any reasonable interpretation of the UN Charter, the Bush (Sr.) administration drove events to a massive escalation of violence. Just the initial phase of that escalation of violence, driving the Iraqis out of Kuwait, is estimated to have cost more than ten times as many lives as Iraq's own actions during the occupation. And that was just the beginning. The internal volatility in Iraq produced by the Gulf War of 1991 led to uprisings in southern and northern Iraq against the government, with a predictably violent response from Baghdad. In southern Iraq, the United States was complicit in Baghdad's suppression of the insurrection.

The violence of the Iraqi government has arisen in a context of violent actors, from armed insurgents to world powers. If we are ever to achieve a rule of law, aggressors must be held accountable for their acts of aggression. That accountability will have to be consistent, whether it is Iraq or the United States or some other country carrying out the aggression. Otherwise there will be no rule of law. The betrayal of the UN Charter by the UN Security Council itself is made obvious by the grotesque and violent response to Iraq's invasion of Kuwait and by the utter failure to apply the law of the Charter in response to the U.S./UK invasion of Iraq.

Economic Sanctions and Iraq's "Hidden Weapons"

After Iraq's retreat from Kuwait, the sanctions were extended on the premise that Iraq might be continuing its development of weapons of mass destruction. But Iraq's WMD programs were effectively terminated by mid-1991. Despite more than seven years of intrusive weapons inspections (1991–98), UN weapons inspectors found no substantive evidence that Iraq was developing WMD. Yet the sanctions continued. A rational person might ask why. A rational answer is that they served functions other than that of a serious arms control measure.

Serious arms control measures must involve multilateral agreements and take into account the legitimate security needs of all parties to the arrangement. Forcing one country to disarm when it faces threats from regional adversaries is not a legitimate arms control measure. When the country is additionally subjected to military assault by the superpower that imposed the disarmament, the problem becomes an obscenity.

The sanctions were, from their inception, well understood to be of a type and severity that would ravage the economy of the targeted country. They represented a state of siege. British and U.S. government efforts to implicate Iraq in WMD production after 1991 were largely designed as propaganda and recently included forged documents, plagiarism, and a series of claims discredited by UN weapons inspectors and by events since the occupation.[7] But for more than a decade the sanctions had an effect on the Iraqi population not unlike weapons of mass destruction, being responsible for hundreds of thousands of deaths, according to international observers. Several United Nations officials resigned in protest against the sanctions.

The sanctions were evidently intended to destroy the Iraqi economy, weaken support for the Iraqi leadership, and thus make it easier to recruit collaborators to overthrow Saddam Hussein. The elimination of Saddam Hussein's government was a consistent U.S. policy objective from August 1990 onward.[8] The Iraqi government was certainly aware that it faced a mortal threat. Exactly how forthright should a government be with its mortal enemies? Saddam's "duplicity and deceit," which served so well as North American propaganda, should be understood in this context. Subsequent events have vindicated the Iraqi government's evasiveness.

By cynically playing on the possibility that Iraq might be developing WMD, the U.S. government was able to recruit the UN Security Council to the siege of Iraq and maintain some public support for the economic sanctions. The effect was a sustained assault not only on Iraq but also on the principles and purposes of the UN Charter, and on international humanitarian and human rights law.

Iraq's "Threat to the Peace"

The legal basis of authority for imposing economic sanctions under certain circumstances is contained in Article 39 and other parts of Chapter VII of the United Nations Charter. Article 39 gives the UN Security Council authority to determine the existence of any threats to the peace and to decide what measures are to be taken in accord with other parts of the UN Charter. Law must be interpreted reasonably, however, if it is to be respected. Iraq's "threat to the peace" must be interpreted in the context of other issues, including the external threats to Iraq's security. Instead, the law was interpreted in a way that served purposes quite different from those expressed in the United Nations Charter.

Even at its peak, Iraq's threat to regional peace was insufficient to defeat Iran, and the threat was rendered marginal simply by removing the external support for it in 1990. For the rest of the decade, the claims of Iraq's "threat to the peace" were themselves largely propaganda for war.[9]

Economic Sanctions and International Law

The legality of the economic sanctions on Iraq after 1991 depended on the argument that Iraq was a "threat to the peace." That argument was fraudulent under any reasonable interpretation of the UN Charter. The economic sanctions on Iraq also failed other tests of legality, including tests under human rights and humanitarian law. Law will be treated with contempt if it is applied inequitably, or if the law is used as pretext to violate the most fundamental principles of the law itself. Both conditions characterize the treatment of Iraq after August 1990. In the case of Iraq, the United Nations Security Council has been subverted to serve the narrowly conceived foreign policy agenda of the United States. That subversion has led to widespread contempt for the Security Council and has undermined credibility of the United Nations itself.[10]

Yet the United Nations Security Council continues to play a constructive role in some situations. When the United States tried to gain its collaboration in the invasion of Iraq, the effort backfired. Iraq unexpectedly agreed to readmit the UN inspectors, despite the past record of espionage and duplicity associated with the inspections. Step by step the inspections began to discredit U.S. and UK claims that Iraq was developing weapons of mass destruction. The time gained in this process allowed the global community's opposition to the war to build, and that made it easier for governments and for the UN Security Council itself to reject collaboration in the U.S. invasion.

The United Nations Security Council is required under Article 24 of the UN Charter to exercise its authority in accord with the purposes and principles of the United Nations. It cannot legally impose economic sanctions or approve the international threat or use of force whenever it likes. Had it approved the U.S. use of force, the invasion would still have been illegal. But in this instance the Security Council upheld the Charter. And that is an important achievement.

Empire or International Law: A Choice

An increasingly global community faces a choice for governance in the decades ahead. The choice is between the norms and structures offered by the international legal system or the norms and structures imposed by empire, the international domination by a powerful state. The problem is clear from Henry Kissinger's statement (*Diplomacy*, 1994): "Empires have no interest in operating within an international system; they aspire to be the international system.... That is how the United States has conducted its foreign policy in the Americas, and China throughout most of its history in Asia." The United Nations Charter and other instruments of international law are based on principles including the sovereign equality of states and purposes including the maintenance of international peace and security. International law provides a pragmatic system for addressing the problems that give rise to international conflict. It has developed in full and fresh awareness of dictatorships, threats to peace, acts of aggression, ethnic and nationalist sources of conflict, and a host of other problems. Contemporary international law recognizes instances in which armed conflict may be justified. It specifies conditions under which the international use of force may be legal, and it provides mechanisms for effective international action to reject breaches of the peace and address threats to peace, while international humanitarian law places constraints on the conduct of war when it does break out.

Each of the two systems, international law and empire, provides a cultural frame of reference. But the cultural domain of empire cannot be universally coherent. Its preference for domination is inherently alien to those it seeks to dominate. Hence the threat and use of force is necessary to maintain "credibility." The military means of maintaining that threat carry an ever-increasing cost, with a steady erosion of economic resources. Hostility to the project simmers and grows, leading to the ultimate decline of empire, after decades or centuries of carnage and waste.

The cultural system of empire is designed to induce deference to power and uses human rights as a stratagem. The standards of international law, by contrast, are designed to constrain excesses of power in order to promote human rights. In the one system, power is the primary value; in the other, human rights. The UN Charter's prohibition on the international threat and use of force, for example, is intended to reduce the resort to war, which unleashes the most fundamental violations of human rights.

Predictably there are sustained efforts to conflate the two systems. Powerful states hope to retain the advantages but escape the constraints of the international legal system. And the public, on whose approval all legitimate power depends, often have a preference for human rights priorities over those of state power. So publicists will often try to represent their government's violations as being consistent with international law, however ridiculous these representations may be.

The legitimacy of empire and its cultural assumptions have been in retreat for more than half a century. Can clever public relations revive enthusiasm for this anachronism? If so, the costs will be staggering. A rule of law offers advantages over a state of lawlessness. It can promote trust, lower the costs of transactions, obviate expenditures on weapons and allow states to direct their resources to basic social needs and promotion of human creative potential. A rule of law can diminish the waste and carnage of the centuries-old pattern in which governments drive their countries toward bankruptcy through military expenditures and destructive international adventurism. Lawlessness, by contrast, encourages violent and criminal behaviour, wastes resources, and leaves the future to the arbitrariness of power and the hazards of chance.

Responsible Citizenship in the Twenty-first Century

Democracy is based on the concept that a government's legitimacy depends on consent of the citizens. Implicit in that concept is another: Citizens are responsible for the policies and practices of their own government, including its atrocities and violations of law.

Governments would prefer that their citizens direct their attention only to the atrocities and violations committed by other governments, in particular a targeted enemy state. A game theorist might notice that perpetually identifying someone else as the source of problems can lead to perpetual animosity, distrust, irresponsibility, and conflict.

As a citizen of the United States and of Canada, I take responsible citizenship to mean engagement in democratic process to bring my own government into compliance with international law. I am familiar with the consumerism, careerism, and cynicism of our culture. I understand the challenges they present to "responsible citizenship," as here defined. I am also closely familiar with a kind of "professionalism" that rejects taking a principled and active role in public affairs, particularly in foreign affairs. Under the terms of this "professionalism," the professional should be politically neutral in public. But there is no such neutrality. By paying taxes we support government policy. The conditions of democracy require that we play a responsible role in shaping that policy. You cannot stand still on a moving train.[11]

Many will reject any personal responsibility of this kind. That is a choice, and the choice has consequences. Lawless violence carries a high cost. It has erosive effects economically, politically, ethically, psychologically, and socially.[12] The human spirit is resilient and tends to tolerate this erosion, even support it or be oblivious to it. And thus we relinquish the far more constructive alternatives that are available. History will continue to present us with the choice of bringing our government's foreign policy into compliance with international law, or not. If we choose wrongly we encourage our collective destruction. But year after year through our silence and passivity, or through more active complicity, we have tolerated or supported major violations of that law. I write this to enable a better informed choice in the future than we have made in the past.

Notes

1   Norman Cousins' book *The Pathology of Power* (New York: W.W. Norton, 1987) eloquently examines some of the problems associated with extraordinary political power.

2   Propaganda for war and other forms of incitement to violence are prohibited under Article 20 of the International Covenant on Civil and Political Rights for good reason. In Rwanda in 1994, such incitement was successful in recruiting many Rwandans to support or even participate in acts of genocide. In North America after 1990, war propaganda recruited public support for the belligerent policies against Iraq that are responsible for hundreds of thousands of deaths, environmental destruction, and a number of other crimes.

3   One of the Iraqi Kurdish leaders who had not supported the insurgency reportedly responded angrily to accusations from the insurgents that he was a traitor: "My villages are still standing and are still wealthy, my people all dress as Kurds, speak Kurdish and have a good life. Look what your nationalism has done for you. Your villages are destroyed, your people have been forcibly resettled, you live in exile and you have nothing left. Why call me a traitor?" The statement is quoted in David McDowall, *A Modern History of the Kurds* (New York: I.B. Taurus, 1996), p. 377. The March 1970 agreement between the Iraqi government and the Kurdish leadership is extensively treated in Chapter 5 of Edmund Ghareeb's *The Kurdish Question in Iraq.*

4   Although the Iraqi aggression against Iran is only briefly mentioned in this essay, it should be emphasized that this carnage simply would not have been possible without the support for that aggression from outside powers. Dilip Hiro's books are outstanding sources on the Iran–Iraq War (*The Longest War: The Iran-Iraq Military Conflict*) and the Gulf War of 1991 (*Desert Shield to Desert Storm: The Second Gulf War*).

5   The Security Council resolution calling for Israel to withdraw from Lebanon was essentially ignored because Israel's violation was in effect supported by the United States.

6   The Iraqi negotiating position for a peaceful withdrawal from Kuwait
     was reported in *New York Newsday* on 3 January 1991. These offers
     generally remained behind the scenes; publicly Iraq was persistently
     refusing to withdraw from Kuwait. The events were well examined in a
     lecture delivered by Noam Chomsky to an audience at Bates College in
     late January 1991.

7   The forged documents, purporting to be from Niger and dating
     from 1999–2000, are referred to in an article from *The Washington
     Post* for 22 March 2003: "CIA questioned documents linking Iraq,
     uranium ore." I retrieved the text of that article through the website,
     www.commondreams.org, which has been an invaluable source for me.
     A useful article on the destructive effects of sanctions is by Mueller and
     Mueller, "Sanctions of Mass Destruction," in the May/June 1999 issue
     of *Foreign Affairs.*

8   A popular revolt, Kurdish independence, and the ascendancy of
     an Islamic state were apparently unacceptable means to the end of
     overthrowing Saddam Hussein. Instead the CIA worked with the Iraqi
     National Congress and the Iraqi National Accord to engineer a more
     controlled outcome. The resulting coup attempts were repeatedly foiled
     by the Iraqi regime.

9   The level of Iraq's "threat" after 1991 was well expressed in an article in
     the *Globe and Mail* of 13 November 1998. Entitled "Hussein Arsenal
     Still Impressive," it carried the subtitle "Although a mere shadow of
     1990's armaments, significant threat exists." In the text, the reporter
     cited an interview with General Binford Peay, who said, "Mr. Hussein
     has been gradually improving the quality of his forces. Although he
     has not managed to even approximate the armament and manpower
     he wielded when his troops invaded Kuwait in 1990, he still poses
     a *significant threat to U.S. pilots who might bomb Iraq*" [emphasis
     added]. In other words, Iraq's capacity for self-defence (its right under
     international law) was still substantial, and that was a significant
     "threat" to future U.S. military plans for Iraq.

10   In commenting on the recent bombing attack on the UN headquarters
     in Baghdad, Denis Halliday, former UN official in charge of the Oil-
     for-Food program in Iraq, noted that "the UN Security Council has
     been taken over and corrupted by the U.S. and UK.... In Iraq, the UN
     imposed sustained sanctions that probably killed up to one million
     people.... It was a great crime against Iraq." Halliday's comments
     following the attack on the UN headquarters were reported by Neil

MacKay, 24 August 2003, *The Sunday Herald* (Scotland), accessed through www.commondreams.org on 24 August.

11 "You cannot stand still on a moving train" is modified from Howard Zinn's phrase, "You can't be neutral on a moving train."

12 An article by Burns Weston, "The Logic and Utility of a Lawful United States Foreign Policy," which appears in *Transnational Law and Contemporary Problems* (Iowa College of Law) 1 (1991): 1–14 points to the destructive power inherent in dismissing international law. The same issue of that journal is devoted to a symposium with a number of other useful essays, including Richard Falk's "Making Foreign Policy Lawful: A Citizen's Imperative" (225–40).

DRUMBEATING FOR WAR? MEDIA VERSUS PEACE AND DEMOCRACY[1]

Robert Hackett

Few Canadians, when they sit down to read a newspaper or watch television news or check the Internet, regard themselves as engaging in an activity relevant to international peace. Yet they may very well be doing just that. We need to ask ourselves if the dominant practices and institutions of public communication share any complicity in the bloody start to the third millennium. What difference do the media make in promoting war or peace? What are the shortcomings of media coverage of life-threatening conflict? These questions and what can be done to improve the shortcomings of the media are the basis of this article.

Media Framing of the War on Iraq in 2003

The prospects of war and peace globally are forged in American media and popular culture as much as anywhere else. Canada's direct access and adherence to American media, especially in television, is omnipresent. Canadian-owned media, both print and broadcast, are dependent on U.S. news sources for copy, television images, and photos. The U.S. media tend to accept the assumptions of empire – that the United States has a right to intervene where its interests are at stake and that it can overthrow governments by force without accountability to international law or the United Nations. The American media can argue that it is their patriotic duty to frame American motives as honourable.

Compared to 9/11, there was, until the invasion of Iraq in March 2003, a greater degree of debate in the American media over military and political options in Iraq, such as the issue of unilateral versus multilateral action. After the United States and Britain invaded Iraq, this debate largely evaporated as the media scrambled to "embed" themselves in flag-waving, soldier-glorifying patriotism. One example of how this played out in Canada is the comparison of coverage of Iraqi civilian casualties relegated to unillustrated back-page copy to the glorifying front-page headlines and photo coverage of the rescue of one American POW. (*Calgary Sun*, 2 April 2003). There are several factors that have contributed to how most American media and many Canadian media framed the post-9/11 "war on terrorism," including the attack on Iraq, resulting in blind spots for readers and viewers.

1. Threatening Events Themselves

Some events, such as the 9/11 terror attacks, readily lend themselves to an either/or, for us or against us, moral discourse. Building on the humanly and morally horrific nature of the event itself, American media coverage offered an emotionally compelling but ultimately dangerously simplistic story line built around the stuff of legend – heroes, villains, and victims. By contrast, the case for war in Iraq required much greater public relations efforts by the Bush administration. The pre-war period, such as the UN weapons inspection process in Iraq prior to invasion, left room for differing viewpoints on what is the right response. But the outbreak of war lent itself to an either/or moral discourse. Previous events, like the Iraqi regime's gas attack on Kurdish civilians fifteen years earlier, were selectively invoked by the administration and enthusiastically amplified by the media. Such a strategy of demonization is a crucial part of how the American media typically present their country's wars to its population. Americans as potential victims (of Saddam's weapons of mass destruction) or heroes of a glorious military is contrasted to Iraq as a site of an evil threat. A sense of being threatened frames the "other" as a demon, allowing all sorts of actions to be justified, including war.

2. The Views of Journalists and Editors and Their Notion of Professionalism

While the sense of threat contributes to a powerful "rally round the flag" effect, accelerating media concentration and commercialization have yielded a corporate culture increasingly hostile to radical dissent, or even to the liberal public service ethos associated with the Walter Cronkite generation.

The 'conservatizing' impact of organizational media culture may be even more relevant to foreign correspondents. Reese Ehrlich, a freelance foreign correspondent writes:

> By the time reporters are ready to become foreign correspondents – a process that can take ten years or more – they understand how the game is played. Becoming a foreign correspondent is a plum job. It's interesting and challenging. You travel frequently and meet international leaders. You may see your byline on the front page. The job has gravitas. And then there's the money.... Money, prestige, career options, ideological predilections – combined with

the down sides of filing stories unpopular with the govern-
ment – all cast their influence on foreign correspondents.
You don't win a Pulitzer for challenging the basic assump-
tions of empire.[2]

With this being the norm for mainstream media reporting, it is not surprising that news stories are framed ideologically in a way in which the media owners, the state, and society in general approve. When renowned U.S. reporter Peter Arnett gave an interview to Iraqi television in which he raised issues about the military strategy of the United States, he was fired.

3. News Routines

Establishment journalism does not want to contextualize news stories, seeking instead to dramatize them in the moral discourse of who is doing what is right and who is doing what is wrong.

With corporate journalism's routine dependence on official sources, elected politicians, and establishment experts, the news stories are framed in a safe and predictable way, however self-serving. That doesn't mean foreign correspondents are mere dupes. They may be well aware of the way their official sources try to manipulate them, and many do question what they are being told. But most do not try to discover what they are *not* being told. And they tend to accept their sources' framing of conflict.

These practices of newsgathering (press conferences held by authorities, etc.) tend to reinforce existing power relations. Oppositional groups are covered but usually as actors rather than as sources. The so-called balanced presentation of an issue usually favours conventional views, reduces complex issues to a for/against format, and allows elite voices to define the limits of discussion.

4. News Organizations' Needs and Policies

Since the 1980s U.S. and Canadian media have undergone massive mergers and consolidation into the hands of a small number of huge companies. For them, journalism is often only a small percentage of revenues. They have big debts to pay off for takeovers, and they want maximum returns from their assets. Except in time of war, cutting back on international news coverage makes economic sense.

In this corporate culture there is de facto censorship within the media. After 9/11, several columnists who offered even mild criticism of Bush were fired. In a country with fewer and fewer media employers, it doesn't take too many such examples for journalists everywhere to feel the chill. The Fox TV news channel in the United States has significantly increased its ratings by its all-out support for the war on terrorism by encouraging its correspondents and presenters to express anger and a thirst for revenge and to present the conflict as a biblical battle of good versus evil. If Fox's stance continues to increase ratings, then other TV channels and even the print media could find themselves under pressure to follow its line.[3]

5. Extra-Media Factors

In the bigger picture, establishment journalism is dependent on the political elite for orientation and the American political elite closed ranks after 9/11. Years of flak from conservatives, convinced despite all the contrary evidence that the media contributed to defeat in Vietnam, have left the press anxious to prove its patriotism. But the press often does not need much pressure because the institutional context of corporate media makes them natural allies of U.S. militarism and capitalist globalization. These giant firms are among the primary beneficiaries of neo-liberal globalization – their revenues outside the United States are increasing at a rapid pace – and the U.S. role as the pre-eminent world power gets them attention. Indeed, the U.S. government is the primary advocate for the global media firms when trade deals and intellectual property agreements are being negotiated. Coincidentally, at the very moment that the corporate broadcasters were drumbeating for America's new war on terrorism, their lobbyists were appearing before the FCC seeking radical relaxation of ownership regulations.[4]

We should recognize the domination of news flows by a handful of commercial, market-driven, corporate enterprises: AOL-Time-Warner, Disney, Bertelsmann, News International. Bias towards commercial propaganda, consumerism, and neo-liberalism is their underlying stance because they are increasingly operating in global markets, undergoing conglomeration, privatization, and hyper-commercialism. Corporate media are integral to the ideology and process of global corporatization.

Those global media help create global public opinion, which can inhibit (albeit selectively) the violation of human rights by particular regimes; but they also promote a culture of consumerism, which arguably breeds inequality, declining sense of community, and ecological devastation. Notwithstanding the Internet and significant regional media production centres (India, Brazil, Egypt), global information flows are still dominated by media corporations based in the developed West. While playing a crucial role outside the

United States, the dominant U.S. media largely insulate their own population from critical foreign perspectives, perspectives that might enable more informed judgments about their own government's policies.

6. Ideology and Culture

It is small wonder that, on the fundamental question of war and peace after 9/11, American media have largely failed to play the role prescribed for them in liberal theory. This theory presents the media as a "watchdog" keeping powerholders accountable, a public forum helping to formulate a democratic consensus between alternatives, and a comprehensive news provider nurturing an informed citizenry. Those failures and blind spots have undoubtedly facilitated the escalating militarization of U.S. foreign policy. And yet in September 2001, American public faith in the media reached the highest levels pollsters have recorded since 1968. What does this dismal combination – democratic failure and public approval – tell us? Media institutions are influenced by, as well as influence, the surrounding political culture. Just as audiences are part of the media system, so journalists are part of that culture.

The media's pre-Iraq war framing of 9/11 meshed well with the dominant frame of America's experience of war, which in turn is related to the foundational myths of American nationhood as the world's singular beacon of freedom, happiness, and opportunity. In the "theology" of American nationalism, 9/11 was not only an atrocity and a tragedy but also an act of sacrilege, one motivated by incomprehensible evil, outside the realm of politics and history. To the extent that audiences and media shared the assumptions of this frame, the U.S. media's construction of the subsequent war in Afghanistan (2002) and then the war on Iraq (2003) was simply a continuation of the ideology of threat and demonization. If the world is wired for violence, media framing of issues in America, the world's hyperpower, is a huge part of the problem.

What about Canadian media? Canada is blessed not to have such a tightly woven foundational national myth of a chosen people in a Manichaean world of good and evil. Canada's identities are more fragmented. As the Quebec sovereignty debate shows, we can't even agree on the territorial or emotional boundaries of the nation. We have five parties in our Parliament and not one and a half like in the United States (Republican and Republican-lite). We have a much stronger public broadcasting tradition in Canada. We have conditions for potentially greater pluralism in our media. But we must not be too smug. Media ownership is more concentrated than it is in the United States, and press barons like the late Israel Asper imposed their own political views on their far-flung properties. Canadian media spread the notion, more or less without challenge, that Canadian military spending is low and that security is lax. The media outrage against professor Sunera Thobani's denunciation of U.S. foreign policy after 9/11 became a lightning rod for those who considered criticism of the U.S. an outrageous affront to a noble ally and friend. She was effectively ostracized in the realm of public discourse, her views put beyond the pale.

What can we do?

There are three points of intervention where media's framing can be challenged. First, there is the role of counter-information. In contrast to the situation in the 1991 Gulf War, there is now a much greater undercurrent of counter-information, which probably contributed to the rejection by global public opinion of the war on Iraq. One factor is progressive websites that have challenged dominant media in terms of setting agendas. This could be one reason that you sometimes see a growing discrepancy between public opinion and media owners' politics. Among these websites are straightgoods.com, rabble.ca, znet, and alternet. In addition to counter-information, the Net is also an amazing organizing tool. The massive peace demonstrations in February and March, even in the United States, came about with relatively little help from corporate media. To be sure, there is an ongoing digital divide. Neither access to the Net nor the ready availability of non-profit-oriented content can be assured. Progressive movements need to be more aware of the political, economic, and policy context of this 'magical' technology and be ready to intervene to protect their access.

The second point of intervention is the alternative journalistic ethos of "peace journalism." It proposes that, in dealing with a life-threatening conflict or issue, it is important for the Canadian media to identify the views and interests of all parties and so avoid dualism. It is wrong to be hostage to one source. A good sense of skepticism is always valuable. Because bias is endemic to human beings, the media has to be self-critical while giving voice to dissident views. When a report on a conflict seeks to talk about common ground and non-violent solutions, it becomes part of the solution. But these approaches run into obstacles – narrative conventions of polarization, commercial biases towards existing knowledge and values and towards affluent, and the ease and cost of accessing U.S.-based transnational news services like Associated Press.

The third point of intervention is media democratization. Since the 1990s, there has been an upsurge in activism directed towards not just using the media as conduits for political messages, but transforming the media themselves into more diverse, accessible, and accountable institutions. This project is fundamental to democracy. Genuinely democratic media would enable each significant social and cultural group to circulate ideas, perspectives, and information in such a way as to reach all other segments of society. That project now needs to be conceptualized globally if we are to promote a productive dialogue rather than a destructive clash of civilizations. The censorship and repression of journalism by the remaining old-style dictatorships of the world clearly need to be addressed. And they are. But we also need a parallel project to challenge the control over public space in the United States and elsewhere by huge transnational media corporations. We may have reached the point where the world's single most important political problem is America's telling stories to the rest of the world without hearing the voices and stories of the rest of the world in return. This engenders frustration and resentment outside the United States and a lack of awareness and sensitivity on the part of Americans to how their government's policies affect the rest of the planet.

In Canadian and U.S. arenas, media democratization takes a number of forms. It means building independent media, outside of state and corporate control. It requires critical media education in schools and beyond. It necessitates continual media monitoring and pressing existing dominant media for better quality and more diverse international news, especially from non-Western sources. Opposition to media concentration and foreign ownership must go hand in hand with the demand for structural change and policy reform of media institutions. Media democratization is also dependent on re-invigorating public service broadcasting, while supporting local, non-profit, and community media. It is important to work on media democratization through advocacy groups and movements and to encourage the peace and anti-global corporatization movements to take on the issue of media democratization as crucial to their own goals.

Notes

1 An earlier and more extensive version of this essay was presented under the title "Media and Life-Threatening Conflict: Is the World Wired for Violence?" as the 2003 Dr. Irma Parhad Lecture at the University of Calgary, 24 March 2003.

2 Reese Ehrlich, *Target Iraq: What the News Media Didn't Tell You* (New York: Context Books, 2003), 17–18.

3 Philip Knightley, *Journalism Studies* (May 2002), 171.

4 Robert W. McChesney, in Barbie Zelizer and Stuart Allan (eds.), *Journalism after September 11* (New York: Routledge, 2002), 91–100.

ON BEING TRAPPED IN THE AMERICAN PARADIGM OF ENDLESS WAR: A PEACE OPTION FOR CANADA[1]

George Melnyk

The War Option

In 2002 I co-edited *Canada and September 11: Impact and Response*. Editing that book convinced me that Canada had entered a serious and very dangerous moment in world history, in which the American paradigm of endless war was the new norm and Canadian foreign relations was its victim. I felt that this new reality had serious repercussions for Canada's distinct civil society and its national identity. In the post-September 11th world, Canada had become identified as a country fully supportive of American imperialist ambition when it gladly sent military forces to invade Afghanistan and overthrow its Taliban regime. At the time, this action was generally applauded by the Canadian population as an appropriate response to the attack on New York's World Trade Center. When the United States continued its imperialist ambitions in 2003 by invading and then occupying Iraq in March and April 2003, Canada refused to join the invading army because the invasion lacked UN support and the public opposition to involvement was significant, particularly in Quebec.

From 1991 (the first attack on Iraq) until 2002 (the invasion of Afghanistan), Canada participated in three American-initiated wars. So why the abrupt about-face in 2003? Had we gone too far in our role as handmaiden? Had the Canadian government reached the proverbial turning point because of its perceived danger in continuing? Or had something else occurred, a new situation arisen? To answer these questions requires dividing the post-World War II Canadian–American relationship on invasions and war into three stages: first prior to 1991, second from 1991 to 2002, and third the current period. Each stage had and continues to have implications for Canadian sovereignty, in particular, and Canadian identity, in general.

From the end of the Korean War (1953), when Canada had joined the United States in a UN-mandated defence of South Korea, until the war to drive Iraq out of Kuwait (1991), Canada did not participate directly in any American military conflict. The Americans fought the Vietnam War for fifteen years, and Canada did not participate other than as a pro-American truce observer. The United States overthrew the elected government of Chile in 1973, defeated the Nicaraguan Revolution in the 1980s, and invaded Grenada and Panama in that same decade, overthrowing their governments, but Canada did not participate. And these regime changes only deal with the Caribbean. The period of the Cold War was one of hot wars between the two superpowers – the United States and the Soviet Union – fought by proxies. While Canada belonged to NATO and was in the anti-Soviet camp, it also showed favour to the Non-Aligned Movement of states that tried to distance themselves from the politics of the Cold War. Since it was the Liberal Party that dominated federal governments from the Korean War to the present, with only two periods of Conservative Party rule, one can conclude that the Liberal Party played an internationalist card in order to give its foreign policy some wiggle room in the face of American dominance and obsession with communism.

Something changed in 1990, when Iraq invaded Kuwait. Canada gave up over three decades of being a semi-independent voice in international relations, devoted to assisting with UN peacekeeping and working to bring bloody conflicts to an end. When Canada joined the UN-sanctioned war on Iraq in 1991, it began a new identity as a military adjunct of the American empire. Canada became a state associated with military intervention, aggression, and war. Participation in this war undid its identity as a middle power proud of its international status as a peacekeeper. From 1953 to 1991, Canada maintained ongoing economic relations with the United States, but it did not provide military personnel to assist the U.S. In fact, during the Vietnam War, Canada protected those Americans who refused to fight. Since 1991 Canada has gone to war another two times on behalf of the United States – in Yugoslavia and Afghanistan, while playing an ongoing naval role in the Gulf region in the post-September 11th U.S. "war on terror."

There are three major factors responsible for this move to war. The first is the collapse of the Soviet Union and Russian communism in 1991 and the end of the Cold War. The second is the U.S.–Canada free trade agreement of 1988 (FTA), followed by the expanded trilateral (United States, Canada, and Mexico) North American Free Trade Agreement (NAFTA) a few years later. These two factors combine the political and the economic in such a way as to push Canada toward American domination in international affairs. The third factor was the invasion of Kuwait by Iraq, which garnered global disapproval and UN condemnation.

With the collapse of the Soviet Union, the world's balancing superpower, Canada's position shifted toward the American side. While the United States and the Soviet Union played an international balancing act, with each power at either end of the teeter-totter, Canada tried to sit in the middle as much as possible. When the U.S. side became the only superpower, Canada slid inexorably toward the U.S. The space for neutrality created by the Cold War shrank appreciably when the diverse world of competing powers and ideologies came to an end. Up to this point, the United States had been loath to wage war directly using its own forces except in the Americas. Other than Lebanon in 1982 and numerous covert operations like Angola, the United States had, instead, used and supported proxy forces, both state and non-state, to fight for its interests in areas outside of South America and the Caribbean. The post-Soviet Union world of the 1990s, with its unopposed American hegemony, proved to be a magnet pulling Canada into American wars against Iraq, Yugoslavia, and Afghanistan. The military balance of power and nuclear deterrence that had once created a world of moving pieces on a chessboard was gone. The Soviet Union and its Eastern European satellites were replaced by the diminished Russian Federation and its NATO-membership and EU-begging former satellites. So Canada found itself face-to-face with a new and threatening geopolitical reality in which there was no real balance to U.S. imperialism.

Canada's integration into the American economy under NAFTA was the second crucial factor pushing Canada toward war. Since the FTA, Canadian exports to the United States have risen to a total of 85 per cent of all exports, while Canada is America's single largest trading partner. The result is dependent production and distribution. Promoted by Canada's business interests and right-wing media, this economic vise has locked Canada into a situation where any attempt at a serious differentiation between the two countries is immediately painted as having negative economic effects on Canadian employment and trade. This was the central focus of the argument denouncing Canada's refusal to invade Iraq in

2003. Because of Canada's dependence on the U.S. economy, the rejection of any integrative measures that the United States demands can turn the border into a problem that has a very serious impact on employment. This economic situation seemed to have sealed our new identity as a supporter of U.S. imperialism around the world, at least until 2003, when Canada's war involvement was obviously reaching a tipping point that the government wanted to avoid.

The third factor that brought Canada into the 1991 war on Iraq (the so-called Gulf War) was its being sanctioned by the UN. With the UN umbrella of Security Council support for driving Iraq from Kuwait, Canada, with its decades-long pro-UN stance, felt it had a perfect excuse to go to war, and since the Americans with their oil interests were keen to ensure the *status quo ante bellum*, the decision was an easy one because no one was asking why this invasion demanded intervention, when other invasions, like those initiated by the Americans in the 1980s, were perfectly fine.

From 1991 to 2002, war was being presented by Canada's right-wing media as a natural condition and something to be proud of. When our "ally" the United States called, we should jump was the message. The media glorified American warrior culture and demanded that Canada emulate it. This was particularly true of the media associated with the pro-American Alliance Party (formerly Reform) position. This position continually harped on Canada's lack of military preparedness for overseas assignments, poor equipment, especially air transport, and inadequate military budgets. It was all part of the pro-American, pro-capitalist, pro-militarist stance of the Canadian Right as it sought to create an American-like society in Canada. According to the Canadian Right, a strong and aggressive military such as that of the United States is the one of the few legitimate activities of the Canadian state (the other is protection of business interests). The only option that makes business sense, according to them, is the war option.

A Brief History of Pro-American War Propaganda

In the context of our NAFTA dependency, pursuing an alternative peace option has serious economic ramifications, but it also has a strong moral dimension. Of course, morality is often thought to be irrelevant to foreign affairs because the concept of "interests" is considered the guiding reality. But when one listens to the rhetoric of war, one finds innumerable moralistic terms being invoked – freedom, democracy, self-determination, human rights, etc. If the war paradigm can invoke morality, so can the peace paradigm. A peace morality would help Canada redefine itself as a nation in the global community as a country that stands outside American imperialism.

A peace identity is based on the principle that *all human life is of equal value.* By adopting this principle, Canada would ensure a permanent, non-warring stance in the world. The moral principle that all human life is of equal value and that glorifying one human life or group over another is wrong may seem self-evident, but, in a culture of war, it is the opposite view that is most widely held and promoted. In the latest war on Iraq, Canadian media generally ignored Iraqi civilian casualties or turned them into relatively faceless statistics of so many hundreds or thousands killed, while American or British casualties were often named and individualized. This is the public morality of warrior states that individualizes and glorifies its own. This rhetorical morality leads Canadians to regret the death of one Canadian in battle while ignoring or cheering on the death of Canada's supposed enemies. When four Canadians were killed by U.S. bombing in Afghanistan in 2002, the media was filled with in-your-face coverage, while the thousands of Afghani casualties were made more or less irrelevant. One Canadian life, as far as Canadians were led to believe, was worth innumerable lives of "the other" – enemy or not.

In the wars that Canada has fought from 1991 to 2002, Iraqis, Yugoslavs, and Afghanis were turned into enemies, although they had never done any harm to Canada. None of these countries had attacked Canada, though some Canadians had died in the World Trade Center attack, and Canada had no substantive geopolitical interests in Iraq, Yugoslavia, or Afghanistan. Endless propaganda encouraged Canadians to support participation in wars that made sense to the Americans because of their interests. Pro-war rhetoric claimed that Canada, as a taken-for-granted ally of the United States, must automatically jump on the war wagon. When the Americans seized control of Baghdad in mid-April 2003, the Canadian media went ballistic with excitement and praise. The Iraqis were war criminals rather than the American and British invaders.

When some human beings are demonized as evil by the media or the state, they are effectively removed from the principle of equality of all human beings. They are no longer human. Since they no longer have lives of equal value to those of "our side," their death and destruction is acceptable. War is always constructed as an either/or situation and as a life and death struggle no matter how puny the opponent. The horrible things that "our" wars have heaped on Iraqi, Yugoslav, and Afghani civilians are justified and even applauded because the foe is portrayed as evil and a monster. Since people know that war is a brutal reality and a scourge on humankind, political propaganda for war needs to be relentless to overcome our natural reluctance to wage war. The easiest way is to dehumanize the enemy while glorifying our actions as morally superior.

The Americans can do no wrong, the argument goes, so we who help them do no wrong.

War is politics by another name. And politics is about power and not about justice. Justifications for war are numerous, especially when the public needs to be led into accepting war against others as legitimate and necessary. The resources of a state in mobilizing public opinion against someone or some group are simply immense. In wartime, all the other problems associated with political leaders are forgotten and their role and identity is turned into something beyond reproach. If political rhetoric and propaganda is not enough, then the state will impose censorship so that only its message of unchallenged patriotism is heard. This message is filled with the binary logic of war in which there are only good guys and bad guys. "They" are the black monsters, and "we" are the knights in shining armour. This attitude leads people to consider the killing of others, however many, as something good or, at minimum, necessary. None of the three countries attacked in part by Canada in 1991, 1999, and 2002 was ever a threat to Canada; yet we attacked them all the same because the Americans had designated them as evil.

If Canada had rejected war and embraced the peace option in 1991, 1999, and 2002, it would have said that it does not buy into the devaluing of human beings by war propaganda. It would have said that it accepts the equal value of all human life, whatever its nationality, race, or religion. It would have made a further political statement that it does not attack other countries unless it is attacked. Embracing offensive war, as Canada did between 1991 and 2002, undermined the concept of the Canadian military as a defensive force.

A review of the American-led wars that Canada joined (it would never have initiated them itself because of its lack of power) is a stark reminder of how the logic of war works. In 1991 Canada joined the United States in an attack on Iraq, which had threatened American control of Middle East oil by invading Kuwait, a dependency of the United States. Canada is not dependent on Middle East oil, so it had no "interest" there other than the claim that it was upholding the authority of the Security Council that authorized a show of force to make Iraq quit Kuwait. Not only did the Coalition's bombing devastate Iraq and cause substantial civilian deaths, the massacre of retreating Iraqi soldiers by American forces is one of the war crimes of the late twentieth century. While Coalition casualties in that war were only a few hundred, half of them from friendly fire, figures for the Iraqi side vary from 30,000 to 100,000 and more. This was basically a bloodbath on the scale of British imperial wars of the nineteenth century against poorly armed opponents. In those days, like today, the deaths on the other side were accepted as normal and perfectly valid.

In 1999 Canada increased its war participation on behalf of the United States by bombing Yugoslavia. This time, there was no United Nations excuse, so Canada played the NATO card. The war was promoted as a war to stop genocide in Kosovo. There was expulsion, an attempt at ethnic cleansing, but no genocide, just the well-oiled propaganda machine of the United States. What was the politics here? It was the politics of ending the rule of the last socialist in Europe, which it did. In the process, over a thousand Yugoslavs died, and Kosovars today are still dying from the cluster bombs that the Americans left behind. But nobody in our society mourns these deaths. Instead we were asked to cheer "our boys" as they bombed and strafed an enemy that didn't have the power to shoot down one enemy plane and in 1999 didn't even have enough fuel to remove its troops and vehicles from Kosovo.

In 2002 Canada again went to war on behalf of the United States. This time, we attacked Afghanistan. Instead of Canadian naval power in the Gulf War and air power in the Yugoslav war, we upped the ante by using ground troops in

Afghanistan. In doing so, we became party to the American violation of human rights and the Geneva Convention on treatment of prisoners of war. We stood behind the United States as it killed over three thousand Afghani civilians in its bombing, and Canada said nothing. We also supported the Americans in the war crime of butchering Taliban prisoners, either directly or through their Northern Alliance allies. The most infamous case was the massacre of prisoners at Mazar-I-Sharif, when hundreds were mowed down. The fight against al-Qaeda was the excuse for barbaric and inhuman treatment of others. If what had been done by the Americans to their opponents (hooding, drugging, and imprisoning in cages) had been done to Americans, there would be a horrendous outcry of barbarism. But doing it to the other side was just fine. This is what happens when you buy into the war option, when you say that the enemy is evil and his life should be extinguished and that whatever we do is acceptable.

How many Canadians cared about the innumerable deaths brought on Iraq by American-forced United Nations sanctions from 1991 to 2003? Very few. These figures are comparable to half a million Canadians being killed. Surely this is a monstrous figure that horrifies us when applied to us. But when applied to Iraqis we are taught to just shrug. We have been taught to consider all and every action against Iraq as moral, civilized, and proper. It is the Iraqi side that is monstrous, not us.

In 2003 Canada said that that the second war on Iraq was wrong because the United Nations had not approved it. It did not say it was evil and motivated by imperialist designs. It did not adopt a moral anti-war principle. It did nothing to have the invasion condemned once it began, and the Liberal government even asked the public and its party members to refrain from criticizing the U.S. invasion so as not to harm relations.

Canada's non-participation in the 2003 Iraq war could be considered a major shift away from the war paradigm, but that would be a false appraisal. Canada's decision was based on four distinct factors. First, it offered the United States thousands of Canadian troops to assist with the occupation of Afghanistan as a substitute for its failure to join the invasion of Iraq – an offer that was readily accepted with the result that now three thousand Canadian troops are now pacifying the country and propping up the American-sanctioned government. Second, it continued to provide naval support in the Gulf for the "war on terror." Third, it was bolstered by the opposition of most of the world plus the UN Security Council that gave the Canadian government enough backbone to say no to participation. Fourth, Canadian public opinion was against participation initially and even after the war was launched a small overall majority supported non-participation. In Quebec the figures against the war and involvement were very high, and with a Quebec provincial election during the war, the federal government's stance boosted the electoral chances of the provincial Liberals. When the federal government was put on the defensive for its non-participation by the attacks of pro-American English Canadian media and interest groups, plus American officials, it did not condemn American and British imperialism, just as the UN did not.

The Peace Option

How would a peace option affect Canada's role in the world community? Let's take the case of Afghanistan. If Canada had sent three thousand people to help to rebuild civil society in that country, instead of sending three thousand soldiers, we would have been a shining example of a new moral stance in the world. If we had worked to build roads, schools, and electrical and medical facilities in an impoverished country, Canada would have become a symbol of hope in international relations. While the Americans continue their "imperialism lite" occupation, no country is making a serious effort to rebuild Afghanistan. Because we don't care about building a civil society in Afghanistan, opium production has return to pre-Taliban levels. Some even say that the United States wants opium production to increase because it encourages drug addiction in Iran and Pakistan. It's what British imperialism did in China a hundred years ago.

If we had said that the Iraqi people, the Yugoslavs, and the Afghanis were human beings of equal value to us, as the peace option claims, then their deaths and destruction would be as unacceptable as our own. We would stop participating in endless American wars. To establish the peace option in Canada, Canadians must first require that its government stop going to war every time the Americans do. With a military force of 1.3 million men and women, near invincibility in military technology, and a war budget exceeding that of the next fifteen countries combined, the United States does not need our military effort except for political reasons. Public opposition to the war on Iraq was a factor in keeping Canada out of war in 2003 because the public read the invasion of Iraq as the same as the invasion of Kuwait. Canadians must further demand that our government stand up for human rights and conventions for international conduct. This would mean more than not going to war. It would mean condemning the United States for its war crimes and its imperialism.

If we are to be seen as objective and just, we must not be seen as apologists for American war crimes and actions, silently tolerating inexcusable conduct.

Canadians must also insist that our government provide alternative forms of action to that of war. When an all-powerful nation like the United States says to the world that either you are for us or you are against us, Canada must reject this intimidation. This division of the world into friend or foe is exactly what the paradigm of war is all about. The peace option values diversity and rejects political monocultures. The Canadian Government needs to improve the climate of international relations today by returning to its former, and now tarnished, peacekeeper image so that it can be counted as a partner in rebuilding war-torn societies. Canadians cannot depend on Canadian business or media or government to make this happen. We have to do it ourselves as citizens concerned about what is happening to our country.

The argument that Canada cannot embrace the peace option because we are dependent on a warrior state for our economic survival is a very powerful one. It appeals to all classes in society from the blue-collar truck driver crossing the border with branch plant products to the businessman on Bay Street watching the NYSE. Economic integration has made the war option the logical one for Canada because it touches on employment and profits. It is economic integration that is the rope (some might say the noose) that binds us to American wars. It is this rope that must be unraveled, slowly, carefully, and inexorably, if the peace option is to ever become a cornerstone of Canadian foreign policy.

A Peace Boycott

Canadians need to launch an economic boycott of the United States until such time as that country drops the paradigm of endless war, which may be a very long time indeed. Through a boycott Canadians will educate themselves about how completely linked our two economies have become. No more buying of American automobiles and other American corporate products and brandname items, nor shopping at American chains in Canada. It would mean no travel to the United States. It would mean no more buying of California vegetables or fruit. In short it would mean no more business dealings by individual Canadians with the American economy. This would result in hardship and increased costs to Canadians who participate. But it is the only way in which we can rid ourselves of the American economic addiction – an addiction that has led us to participate in American wars.

I am proposing a Gandhi-inspired model in which the supporters of a boycott bring hardship upon themselves. Even if every Canadian joined the boycott, the economic impact on the United States would be modest, while the economic impact on Canadians would be massive, even revolutionary. Only if citizens in other countries joined in this boycott would the United States pay some economic attention, and the possibility of that happening is very slim, if non-existent. But the political message of a boycott would be powerful threat to the United States. Boycott U.S.A. would affirm Canadian independence and the peace option in international affairs.

Because a majority of the Canadian public has been convinced of the value of the U.S. relation, the supporters of an economic boycott would be a tiny minority. So the impact of the boycott on the United States would be marginal, if any, unless of course the boycott became a popular movement. Boycott U.S.A. would have to view itself as a moral movement whose profile in the Canadian consciousness would be greater than its economic impact because of its principles. The movement would have four organized levels, as well as an unorganized level. The unorganized level involves anyone who wishes to boycott the United States economically to as little or great a degree as they privately desire. The organized levels include the lowest level of associate boycotters, who support the movement but participate in an informal and ad hoc manner, picking and choosing what they wish to boycott. The level above associate are the "lite" boycotters, who adhere to a program that has the least hardship associated with it. The next level is the "regular" boycott, while the highest level is "total" boycott. The movement would set the standards for each level of boycott and support people involved in a variety of formal ways. The movement would also promote the peace boycott concept nationally and establish mechanisms to assist people by providing information on American products, services, and companies while offering alternative non-American sources and group support. The boycott would not preclude other activities to end Canada's participation in the American war machine.

Participation in Boycott U.S.A. reminds Canadians how easily we have been drawn into the dark crusade of ever more war, murder, destruction, and even annihilation. If Canada is to regain its former peacemaker role, it needs a population that is active in resisting war, and Boycott U.S.A. is a fundamental expression of a new direction. Just as our participation in American wars has weakened Canada's ability to represent alternatives to war, a failure to provide alternatives encourages more war and human suffering. If Canada had accepted the principle of every life being of equal value as public policy, we would be one of the few nations in the world on the path of creating peaceful reconciliation. We cannot expect the state or capitalism or the media to embrace the peace option. This is an initiative of the citizenry – as were the great anti-war demonstrations of February and March 2003. These demonstrations did not stop the invasion and conquest of Iraq nor the culture of endless war that the U.S. government embraces, but they did show that only people, inside and outside the United States, can offer an alternative that is just and peaceful. Boycott U.S.A. would show Canadians and the many Americans opposed to war-mongering that democracy is strengthened by peaceful opposition. In the end, working for the peace option makes Canadians stronger as individuals and as a nation. In terms of Canadian sovereignty, the peace option is the only patriotic alternative.

1 This article is based on a presentation made at the *Trading in Violence/Building for Peace: Challenging the Corporate State*, Annual Parkland Institute Conference, University of Alberta, 15 November 2002. It has been expanded, updated, and revised to take into account the invasion of Iraq in 2003.

OBSERVING: INTERNATIONAL PERSPECTIVES ON CANADA'S ROLE IN THE NEW EMPIRE

SQUANDERED RESPONSIBILITY:
CANADA AND THE DISARMING
OF IRAQ

Scott Ritter

The Canadian reputation regarding its support of the United Nations is well deserved. This reputation has been paid for with the service and sacrifice of its armed forces, who participated in many peacekeeping operations around the world. In contrast, Canadian participation in perhaps the boldest experiment in disarmament ever attempted in the history of the United Nations – the elimination of Iraq's weapons of mass destruction programs – is more an accident of history than design.

Canada served as a non-permanent member of the United Nations Security Council when the operative resolution regarding Iraqi disarmament, 687 (1991), was passed, and as such earned a seat on the Special Commission established by that resolution to oversee the implementation of its provisions. Headed by an Executive Chairman appointed by the Secretary General, who reported directly to the Security Council, the fifteen Commissioners of the Special Commission provided advice and expertise but had little influence over executive decision-making. The executive chairman turned to the Office of the Special Commission for the day-to-day implementation of the Council's disarmament mandate. The Office of the Special Commission was where the administrative and functional expertise regarding weapons of mass destruction and disarmament affairs resided, and it is where the technical and operational aspects of the weapons inspection process were directed. The influence of the Commissioners was more indirect than direct, reflecting their status as representatives of nations serving on the Security Council. However, representative membership on the Commission did not change with the evolving makeup of the Security Council. Once appointed to the Special Commission, Canada retained its seat even when its term on the Security Council expired.

The original intent behind the formation of the Special Commission was the maintenance of a direct link between it and the Security Council. Hardly anyone anticipated a situation that had the work of the Special Commission lasting more than six months. As the reality of the difficulty entailed in bringing Iraq's weapons of mass destruction programs to heal became apparent, the envisioned six-month mission expanded into a year and beyond. The link between the Special Commission and the Security Council became increasingly diluted as the membership of the Security Council changed over time. Canada, like many nations, found itself participating in an advisory capacity to an organ of a Security Council in which it no longer had status. The result was an increasing Canadian detachment from the process of disarmament in Iraq because of dependence on specialists at the tactical level of inspection operations and an indifference concerning the strategic aspects of the commission's work.

The ramifications of this slide into irrelevancy has been tragically exposed by the inability of the Canadian government to formulate a coherent position regarding Iraqi compliance with its disarmament obligation based upon independent assessment and analysis. Instead, the Canadian government was compelled to rely upon information of questionable objectivity and reliability provided by the United States. As a result, when the United Nations could have most used an independent and credible voice to provide alternative analysis and solutions to the Iraqi crisis other than the path of war being pushed by the United States and Great Britain, Canada was mute. True, Canada opposed the war. But its opposition came very late in the process, was inconsistent in its substance, and lacked any sound alternative solution. Given the commitment of the United States to a unilateral policy of regime removal in Iraq that deviated from the mandate of disarmament set forth by the Security Council, the subordination of Canadian Iraq policy formulation to the United States is not only embarrassing but tragically so, especially when one considers that Canada had been given an historic opportunity to play a completely different and more independent role in the affairs of the Special Commission. How Canada squandered that opportunity needs to be studied by those who make and oversee foreign policy in Canada today so that any lessons drawn from this unfortunate episode of neglect will not be repeated in the future.

The opportunity granted to Canada in 1991 came in the form of three positions of considerable influence filled by Canadian officials. The first, that of a Commissioner of the Special Commission, was filled by Ron Clemenson, a retired Royal Canadian Air Force officer with a specialization in aerial surveillance. The second was the position of Chief of the Information Assessment Unit, an intelligence cell created within the Office of the Special Commission in the fall of 1991 in response to Iraq's inadequate declarations concerning its weapons of mass destruction programs, its obstruction of the work of weapons inspectors in Iraq, and ongoing concealment activity designed to hide proscribed materials and programs from the Special Commission. In an effort to diversify the national composition of the Office of the Special Commission, as well as retain the ability to interface with the United States on matters pertaining to the sharing of classified intelligence, the executive chairman requested that Canada fill this position with seconded staff (someone who works for the Special Commission but is paid for by the providing government). Lieutenant-Colonel Geoff St. John was selected for this assignment and assumed his post in November 1991.

The third position was on the staff of a shadowy intelligence organization known as "Gateway," run out of a United States Central Intelligence Agency facility in Bahrain. Although not part of the United Nations or directly affiliated with the Special Commission, "Gateway" was a critical component in the chain of intelligence support and analysis associated with the work of UN weapons inspectors inside Iraq. Bahrain was home to the Special Commission's field office, where inspection teams assembled and were trained prior to being dispatched to Iraq. Post-mission debriefing of inspection teams, perhaps the most important source of raw intelligence data concerning Iraq's disarmament status, was likewise conducted in Bahrain. The "Gateway" facility and staff were provided by the CIA to the Special Commission as a vehicle for the provision of sensitive intelligence support to the inspectors and gradually expanded into an all-purpose intelligence resource for the inspectors where pre- and post-mission work was conducted in a secure environment. Canada, together with Australia and the United Kingdom, was invited by the United States to participate in the "Gateway" operation, and the Canadian Secret Intelligence Service (CSIS) assigned officers on a rotational basis to Bahrain for that work.

Canada also made significant contributions to the weapons inspections themselves, providing Explosive Ordnance Disposal (EOD) teams who carried out extremely dangerous work inside Iraq, safeguarding the other members of the inspection team who were oftentimes operating in areas inundated with unexploded munitions, including unstable cluster bomb units left over from the 1991 Gulf War. These EOD personnel also doubled as site exploitation specialists, assisting the inspection teams by serving as ground security and by providing documentation exploitation and aerial observers (riding in German-provided CH-53 helicopters to provide overhead surveillance and observation support to teams working on the ground). The result of this considerable scope and depth of involvement in the work of the Special Commission was that Canada was in a position to participate in every phase of the inspection cycle, from political support to inception, implementation, and post-mission analysis and feedback.

Due to the nature of my own assignment and responsibilities with the Office of the Special Commission, I was in a unique position to observe all of this. I first met Ron Clemenson in September 1991, when I was brought into the Office of the Special Commission to assist in setting up the Information Assessment Unit (Lt. Col. St. John assumed command in November 1991). Ron Clemenson was very keen on assisting the Special Commission in developing aerial surveillance monitoring strategies for Iraq. The Information Assessment Unit was tasked with overseeing the U-2 high altitude surveillance program. The United States provided the U-2 spy plane and flew it on behalf of the Special Commission, who determined the reconnaissance targets and received the imagery product, together with imagery exploitation support from the CIA.

Ron and I met on numerous occasions to discuss the integration of the U-2 into a wider, more independent program of aerial monitoring of Iraq. Lt. Col. Geoff St. John and I worked together for the entire duration of his assignment to the Special Commission, defining the role and mission of the Information Assessment Unit and supervising the transition of that unit from a simple analytical support cell into a genuine international intelligence service that not only assumed primacy in the international community regarding intelligence analysis regarding Iraq's weapons of mass destruction but also became involved in liaison with intelligence services around the world and developed its own independent multi-source intelligence collection capability. As an operational planner and later chief inspector for weapons inspection teams, I not only helped define the inter-operability between the Special Commission and "Gateway" but was directly involved in participating in the process of intelligence support conducted there. This put me in regular contact with the CSIS personnel assigned to "Gateway." And, as an inspector, I had the honour and privilege to serve with the fine representatives of the Canadian Armed Forces who were seconded on a regular basis as members of Special Commission inspection teams on duty inside Iraq.

The role and influence of the IAU in shaping the work of the Special Commission cannot be underestimated. Not only was the IAU the source for the fundamental assessments regarding Iraqi compliance, but it was also the originator of every innovation in terms of intelligence collection and operational employment of inspection teams. The IAU was behind large document search inspections, the incorporation of helicopter-borne cameras into the Special Commission's aerial surveillance program, the tactical use of U-2 imagery, utilization of ground-penetrating radar in the search for underground facilities, the use of communications intercept teams embedded with the weapons inspectors to detect Iraqi command and control of concealment activities, the debriefing of Iraqi defectors, and other, more sensitive programs. With a Canadian at the helm of the IAU, Canada was in a unique position not only to be aware of every aspect of the Special Commission's disarmament work but to influence how this work was carried out. Canada has long prided itself as a defender of the legitimacy of an impartial and objective United Nations. Lt. Col. St. John's tenure as chief of the IAU epitomized this standard. He worked hard to build a viable, independent intelligence capability for the Special Commission, one that was dedicated to the Security Council's disarmament mandate. He struggled to overcome not only Iraqi duplicity and obstruction but also the sustained efforts of the United States to undermine his efforts. The regime removal policy of the United States regarding Iraq's president meant that the United States only viewed the weapons inspection mandate of the Special Commission as useful insofar as it facilitated the containment, destabilization, and eventual elimination of the Saddam regime. While much of the world's attention was focused on the struggle between weapons inspectors and Iraq, an equally titanic battle to preserve the integrity of the Special Commission's mandate was waged between the IAU and CIA over the independence of the Special Commission's intelligence functions and capabilities. Lt. Col. Geoff St. John was at the forefront of this struggle and deserves great credit for persevering in the cause of the United Nations while under tremendous pressure to do otherwise.

Ron Clemenson was also a champion of independence and viability in regard to the Special Commission, especially as it pertained to imagery collection and analysis in support of inspection operations. In the spring of 1993, when the Special Commission, through the IAU, was exploring the expansion of its in-country aerial surveillance operations beyond the rudimentary helicopter-borne Aerial Inspection Team (AIT) to a more robust Aerial Inspection Group (AIG) that incorporated the AIT, a Russian AN-30 multi-sensor collection platform, and Iraqi Mirage F-1 aircraft flying under UNSCOM control, Ron Clemenson provided critical support in obtaining a qualified officer from the Canadian Air Force to be seconded to the Special Commission to head up AIG operations inside Iraq. This type of support was the ideal utilization of the members of the Special Commission. While the Commission itself met only twice a year to discuss the work of the inspectors in Iraq, individual commissioners were repeatedly called upon by the Office of the Special Commission to intercede on behalf of the inspectors with their respective governments on matters pertaining to support. Ron Clemenson's intervention on behalf of the AIG is representative of this.

With Canadian support leading the way in terms of intelligence and aerial surveillance operations inside Iraq on behalf of the Special Commission, and with Canadian personnel embedded on almost every ground inspection of note, the CSIS representative at "Gateway" was in a position to be involved in the assembly of a comprehensive picture of the overall disarmament effort being implemented by the inspectors. Given the senior level of Canadian representation in critical nodes of the Special Commission's inspection efforts, the potential of CSIS to influence and shape implementation of Iraq's disarmament exceeded that of even the United Kingdom. Additionally, the ability of the CSIS "Gateway" representative to provide first-hand intelligence reporting on the intimate details of the Special Commission's work inside Iraq meant that Canadian decision-makers would have access to all the data necessary to formulate effective policy in support of the United Nation's disarmament mandate.

Sadly, the Canadian government squandered this unique position. By the summer of 1993, the Canadian government no longer held its seat on the Security Council, and interest in supporting the work of the Special Commission waned as other fiscal priorities emerged that competed with those resources then being dedicated to Iraq's disarmament. Lt. Col. Geoff St. John's period of assignment expired in May 1993, and the Canadian Government chose neither to extend Lt. Col. St. John nor to provide a replacement. Canada lost its seat at the head of the IAU. Likewise, Canada stopped filling its CSIS position at "Gateway" on a full-time basis. Inspection teams would thereafter be dispatched and debriefed from the "Gateway" facility in Bahrain without any direct Canadian involvement. Not only did Canada lose its ability to influence inspection decision-making, but the Canadian Government was put in the position where it became dependent on intelligence reporting from the United States and the United Kingdom. Given the competing and contradictory policy objectives of the United States (regime change versus disarmament), this was not a good position for Canada to be in, if it was in fact serious about an independent, objective United Nations.

The dramatic reduction in Canadian presence and support for the Special Commission severely impacted Ron Clemenson's role as commissioner as well. Without major backing from the Canadian Government, the AIG initiative fizzled and with it Mr. Clemenson's influence as a commissioner. My last impression of Mr. Clemenson in that role was in November 1997, during an emergency meeting of the Special Commission, when his comments on the imagery collection and analysis conducted by the IAU in support of a series of controversial inspections reflected his then isolation from and lack of knowledge regarding the work of the Special Commission. When I compared that performance with the more dynamic interventions that he made in the period 1991–93, the contrast was considerable.

The work of the Special Commission underwent dramatic transformation between the years 1994 and 1998. Major events and developments took place, which shaped the commission's disarmament mandate. These included the Iraqi acknowledgment of a biological weapons program in April 1995; the defection of Hussein Kamal (Saddam Hussein's son-in-law and mastermind behind Iraq's weapons of mass destruction programs) in August 1995; the interception of Russian missile parts in Jordan in November 1995 (and the unspoken role of the Special Commission's relationship with Israeli intelligence in that and other IAU-affiliated operations); the counter-concealment inspection campaign targeting Saddam Hussein's security apparatus which started in 1996 and continued through 1998; sensitive site inspection modalities agreed upon in June 1996; communications intercept operations carried out by the Special Commission from 1996 to 1998; the fracturing of relations between the Special Commission and Iraq in 1997 and 1998 and the corresponding demise of the Special Commission's relations with the United States. All took place without Canada's direct involvement or knowledge.

The demise of the Special Commission as an inspection organization in 1998 took Canada by surprise with resulting uncertainty how next to proceed. The slide into policy impotence was evident as early as the spring of 2000, when I met with a Canadian Government representative at the Canadian embassy in Washington, D.C. This representative all but acknowledged that Canada was completely beholden to the United States for information regarding Iraq's disarmament status and as a result was unable to meaningfully influence United Nations policy formulation, which was then heavily influenced by the position of the United States and United Kingdom. The level of American influence was still very much in evidence when I travelled to Ottawa in June 2002 for meetings with Canadian defence and intelligence specialists, as well as Canadian Parliamentarians. The Canadian government had no ability to independently comment on the situation in Iraq and was forced to simply parrot the position of their more powerful U.S. ally. This lack of independence of data manifested itself most recently and tragically when Canada proved incapable of mounting any serious opposition to the United States' drive towards war with Iraq. Despite a Canadian population overwhelmingly opposed to war with

Iraq, the Canadian government proved to be capable of doing nothing more than voicing qualified words of caution.

When one considers the unique position Canada found itself in in 1993, when it 1) headed the Special Commission's intelligence function, 2) had a Canadian commissioner who was a player of note in the affairs of the Special Commission, 3) had an intelligence officer deeply embedded in the centre of intelligence data collection efforts carried out by the CIA, and 4) contributed Canadian inspectors involved throughout the scope of disarmament activities inside Iraq, the fact that Canada found itself reduced to the status of impotent observer as the Iraq situation devolved in 2002–03 is inexcusable. Given Canada's stated goal of being a defender of the United Nations Charter and the rule of international law contained within it, this inability on the part of Canada to influence events of such global importance represents not only a squandered opportunity but, more critically, a gross dereliction of international duty.

While nothing can be done to undo the damage caused to the United Nations Charter as a result of the U.S. invasion of Iraq in the spring of 2003, maintenance of the Charter and the UN as a viable force in preserving global peace and security in the years to come can only come about when the UN's individual members reflect on where they went wrong in defending the Charter and what they can do in the future to improve upon their respective records. Given the missed opportunities afforded Canada during the decade of inspections in Iraq, there is much to be discussed in Ottawa today.

DOGGONE DIPLOMACY? THE IRAQ WAR, NORTH AMERICAN BILATERALISM, AND BEYOND

Imtiaz Hussain

Introduction

The U.S. battlefield strategy of "shock and awe" also rocks diplomacy! Against a post-9/11 "with-us-or-against-us" U.S. attitude, countries economically dependent on the United States make reluctant foreign policy choices! Whether these countries transacted with pre-war Iraq as Russia and Syria allegedly did, hindered military movements like Turkey, or opposed the war as Canada and Mexico boldly opted to, each faces a "damned-if-I-do; damned-if-I-don't" predicament.[1] Accenting Mexico's and Canada's cases, I argue how and why twenty-first century diplomatic imperatives of other countries also carry symptoms of this malaise!

Mexico's telltale experiences were ill-timed. On the eve of 9/11, President Vicente Fox Quesada not only got away by proposing the unthinkable – relaxing border controls for U.S.-bound migrants – but also assertively seating Mexico on the Security Council as a non-permanent member as part of his activist foreign policy. Confusion in formulating a coherent UN Iraq policy approach made Mexico's third Security Council appearance both unlucky and ironic. The French/Russian threat to veto UN Resolution 1441 if a military ultimatum was imposed upon Iraq found Mexico's sympathy but also revived memories of Mexico's staunch opposition to adopting the veto itself as an instrument in 1946, when it first took a Security Council seat.[2] Mexico's second stint in the Security Council, under President José Lopéz Portillo during 1980–81, sought to balance rather than embrace U.S. interests. By reversing this order, instead of strengthening Mexico's special relationship with the United States, as was actually intended, Fox discovered its seamy side. His own foreign policy incongruencies paralleled the ups and downs of UN Resolution 1441 itself.

The Ghost of UN Resolution 1441

Mexico's foreign policy activism under Fox literally meant putting all his eggs in the U.S. basket! One casualty was Mexico's remarkable historical relationship with Fidel Castro's Cuba. Yet, by the time Resolution 1441 was tabled in autumn 2002, Mexico had shifted from the centre of George W. Bush's foreign policy radar to a distant blip. Fox and Foreign Secretary Jorge Castañeda were left with three options: (a) unambiguously support the United States, like Great Britain's Tony Blair and Jack Straw; (b) passively support non-interventionism, thus swaying with public opinion; or (c) actively promote multilateralism over U.S. unilateralism, whatever the consequences. Mexico's Cuban *volte-face* after Fox's election in 2000 pursued the first track and even erroneously assumed the United States would drop barriers on Mexican migrants as a *quid pro quo*.[3] Yet, even before 9/11, the U.S. Congress was resistant. The second route of passivity just did not mesh with the styles of either Fox or Castañeda but briefly explained reality anyway; and the third option became increasingly impossible, given Mexico's dependence on the United States and its history of introversion with little or no experience in high-voltage international politics.

Five actual Mexican responses can be identified during the Iraq crisis at the UN, as Table 1 profiles. First, Mexico sought to act as a balancer until 8 November 2002. Whereas France sought more discretion and time for the UN inspection process, the United States arm-twisted Security Council members to put Iraq on a short deadline. Mexico sympathized with the former but fell prey to U.S. pressure. Second, Mexico's shift to neutrality when Hans Blix reported on the progress of the weapon's inspection process on 27 January 2003 was built on a three-tiered approach: leave the issues to the protagonists – France, Germany, Britain, and the United States;[4] officially urge Iraqi compliance, which appeased the United States; and simultaneously magnify the role the UN should have to a wary public. On the positive side, this thwarted charges of Mexico abdicating its Security Council responsibilities to an equally wary South America; played to public opinion; and permitted diplomatic piggy-backing. On the negative side, it exposed the constraints of dependence on the United States.

Mexico moved from second-stage neutrality to third-stage ambiguity after Blix's second report on 14 February 2003. As it scrambled to define a coherent position, other Security Council members scurried in three different but decisive directions: support for continued UN inspection, rally behind a U.S.-led invasion, or play France and the United States off for economic rewards. Under new foreign secretary Luís Ernesto Derbez, Mexico's ambiguity meant supporting the UN and appeasing U.S. interests by urging Iraqi compliance. Meanwhile, a British-Spanish-U.S. initiative for a second resolution found support from only Bulgaria, while China, France, Germany, Pakistan, Russia, and Syria remained opposed, leaving Angola, Cameroon, and Guinea in search of the highest economic bidder. As Chile pursued a compromise initiative of its own, Mexico faced its worst Security Council nightmare, enduring diplomatic isolation in the process.

Inconsistent domestic and external developments produced a fourth Mexican response of abnegation after Blix's 7 March report, which paved the way for its fifth response of officially opposing the U.S. war declaration. Fox shifted from ambiguity towards subordinating the U.S. call to arms because of growing domestic disenchantment and restlessness. When the Bush–Blair 16 March Azores decision to wage war eliminated even the faintest hope of a no-border migration deal with the United States, Fox had no choice but to be counted among the opponents. Consequently, Mexico's routine turn to preside over the Security Council during the month of April was tantamount to a lost opportunity: It could not pursue any initiative in peacekeeping, balance U.S. interests, coattail its northern neighbour, or espouse other widely felt needs to its fellow members. All that was left for it to do was to call for supporting humanitarian issues, even then *a posteriori*. The resultant message is significant: Without diversifying economic and political partners, when push turns to shove, the weaker partner is condemned, often twice over – first for lack of principles such as loyalty and second for a supposed lack of realism about the consequences to itself.

Extending the Argument to Canada

To what extent is this "damned-if-I-do; damned-if-I-don't" argument valid for the other U.S. neighbour, Canada? A comparative survey of Canadian responses to Resolution 1441 is insightful. Like Mexico, Canada is a U.S. neighbour, and under greater U.S. scrutiny for being an alleged gateway to would-be terrorists. It is not part of the current Security Council.

Table 1: Mexico's Evolving Security Council Responses

Thresholds:	Mexico's Responses:	Plausible Considerations:	Possible Consequences:
1. Deliberations leading to UN Resolution 1441 (October–November 2002):	Balancing role sought: sympathy for French position, reluctant support for U.S. position	External factors more evident than internal: Identity with France and Russia more symbolic than substantive, but still more influential than domestic considerations	Castañeda's resignation one of the many dominoes to fall, altering atmosphere for Mexican foreign policy-making
2. U.S. challenges UN and Blix's first report (27 January 2003):	Shift to neutrality, prompted by Blix report, and based on three considerations	External factors still more evident than internal: Continued identity with France, this time with Germany and Russia	Exposes constraints of dependence on U.S.: abdication of Security Council responsibilities
3. U.S. brinkmanship within the context of Blix's second report (February 2003):	Neutrality turns into ambiguity: new foreign secretary supports UN role but appeases U.S.	Security Council torn in three directions – Mexico, uncomfortable in any, faces *unsplendid* isolation	Virtual isolation in the wake of GB-Spain-U.S. proposal for second UN resolution
4. Tripartite resolution amidst the most promising Blix report against war (first week of March 2003):	Policy of abnegation	External and domestic interests collide: electoral calendar enters foreign policy calculations	Public opinion unconvinced; UN-based approach not delivering
5. Road to war (16 March Azores summit and after):	Official opposition to U.S. war declaration; call for mobilizing humanitarian support	External factors outweigh domestic factors for the short-term, but electoral accountability casts long-term shadow	Lost opportunities: principles abandoned, but interests trampled

Although its final word on Resolution 1441 was identical to Mexico's, the route taken was not similar. How Canada tossed and turned between neutrality and ambiguity echoed Mexico's predicament. Although balancing was not attempted, Canada differed most radically from Mexico because it was partially engaged militarily. Jean Chrétien's "Canada will not participate" affirmation in the House of Commons after the Azores die had been cast was true to the bone: Canada refrained from a combat role.

Yet other roles lay in waiting in terms of preparatory work, psychological boost, and participating in the broader campaign against terrorism as well as supplementing Operation Iraqi Freedom. However, Canada jumped in with both feet: It deployed three naval vessels to join the U.S.-led coalition fleet in the region, dispatched twenty-three military officers to parley with their U.S. counterparts in the Qatar command-control centre from February, provided thirty-odd AWAC officers for sorties in or near the Iraqi combat zone, desired to be part of any post-war reconstruction plans and provide post-war security forces, and currently supervises, with over two thousand soldiers, the International Security Assistance Force (ISAF) in Afghanistan. On the other hand, Canada and Canadians cannot forget how four of their soliders were killed by friendly U.S. fire in Afghanistan – worse still, how the culprits escaped court-martial. At the same time, Canada worked diligently with UN Security Council members both before Resolution 1441 was unanimously passed in November 2002 and after. When a breakdown looked likely in February 2003, its UN ambassador, Paul Heinbecker, canvassed the ten non-permanent members with a bridging deadline proposal. This didn't work, and probably none of the representatives were listening anyway. As a previous section indicated, their preferences and preoccupations were elsewhere. Lost in this maelstrom was a Canadian-Mexican opportunity, if not to slow its preponderant neighbour, then to initiate an independent, long-term bilateral compact.

Far from being chimerical, a thriving Canada–Mexico political understanding may become the most feasible exit option for both from their utter U.S. dependence. To be sure, neither of these relationships with the United States are drastically Machiavellian: Both have enjoyed spells of special status, and the United States did not force either into any commercial engagement. Just as Brian Mulroney proposed a free trade agreement to the United States at the 'Shamrock' Summit, September 1986, Carlos Salinas de Gortari did likewise in Davos, February 1990.[5] The Mexican proposal, interestingly, was fully rejected by Canada – for six months or so. Since then, relations have spiralled at both societal and state levels, as Chrétien himself acknowledged at the 450th anniversary of Mexico City's Universidad Nacional Autonoma de México in late February 2003.[6] He highlighted the million-or-so Canadians who visit Mexico each year, more than ten thousand Mexican students studying in Canadian institutions of higher learning, over four hundred agreements bringing universities of the two countries together, and growing cultural exchanges between them, for example, Canada's strong participation in Mexico's annual Cervantino Festival. Canada had become Mexico's second largest trading partner, Mexico Canada's fourth best customer, and both currently accounting for almost one-third of the U.S. market. In reality, both bilateral trade and investments are small: Bilateral Canadian-Mexican trade accounts for less than 5 per cent of Mexico's overall transactions, and European investments far outweigh Canadian, especially in the lucrative, denationalized banking sector. Without expansion in both areas, diversification possibilities remain limited; and formidable barriers await such expansion anyway: A large portion of exports to the other could more easily be marketed in the United States; both naturally gravitate towards the United States, which is partly why a "damned-if-I-do; damned-if-I-don't" predicament prevails; and, as a huge tract of land between the two, the United States remains a natural barrier to bilateral transactions between the two countries

Argument in Even Broader Light

Although the degree varies, helplessness against the United States is a common Mexican and Canadian fraility. What specific features of their "damned-if-I-do; damned-if-I-don't" helplessness may be of general relevance to other countries, or even predict their own specific futures? Four specific issues are explored before identifying some general features:

First, domestic politics influence foreign policy outcomes. For Fox this involved electoral considerations, while for Chrétien it was his retirement. With the public overwhelmingly against a war before Mexico's mid-term legislative elections in July 2003, Fox pragmatically trimmed his external interests to suit domestic realities. It didn't help, since his PAN party lost anyway, and precisely because external interests in the United States had soured: U.S. unilateralism and recession prevented much needed domestic reforms.[7] Similarly, Chrétien's greater manoeuvrability in opposing the war, stemming to some degree from his impending departure from politics, not only jeopardized relations with the United States, but also left other Canadian sectors unhappy, especially the business community and media. Paul Martin's prime ministership suggests a return to an antebellum Canadian–U.S. camaraderie.[8]

Second, deep trade dependence on the United States also reduces foreign policy options and initiatives of both neighbours. Although any significant U.S. retaliation against Mexico or Canada would undoubtedly prove costly for the United States too, given the high degree of economic complementarity in both bilateral relations, the United States is less exposed and vulnerable than its two neighbours by virtue of its greater size and diversity in partners. Nevertheless, North America's hitherto win–win progression under NAFTA is expected to be negatively affected, if not by the Iraqi fallout, then by a recessionary U.S. economy.

Third, an oppositional foreign policy doesn't help if the goal is to strengthen ties with the United States. Fox's strong support of democratization and liberalization, two core U.S. ideologies, while reducing Fox's personal political fortunes domestically, had little currency in a belligerent U.S. Canadians could also learn from Pierre Trudeau's ill-fated Third Option.[9] Pursued vigorously during the 1970s to diversify economic partners beyond just Great Britain and the United States, it simply could not overcome the U.S. gravitational pull on Canadian trade and investment. As its failure was being recognized in the early 1980s, the MacDonald Report also found the Canadian–U.S. economic relationship to be the springboard of Canadian economic growth.

Finally, the replacement of long-cherished principles or constitutional provisions by pragmatic amendments is unlikely to always bring desired results. Fox's plans to eventually privatize such sensitive sectors as electricity and petroleum are also likely to leave him embattled for the remainder of his tenure.

Four features of general relevance emerge from the discussions: (a) the nature of *special* relations with the United States amidst a global crusade; (b) the growing state-society disjuncture; (c) balancing reciprocal domestic-external determinants; and (d) adjusting long-cherished principles to pragmatic needs.

Ordinary rather than Extraordinary

How Mexico's and Canada's special U.S. relationships broke down alerts us against taking them for granted or as a permanent feature of the political landscape for several reasons: policy divergences are as routine as convergences; special relationships are not immune to business swings, which generate even sour moods; the presence of resilient *binational* populations in all three North American countries complicate post-9/11 economic liberalism more than they help; and embedded asymmetry softens neither the growing dependence of Canada and Mexico on the United States nor the plight both countries may face under difficult circumstances.

Prior to 9/11, Fox's relationship with Bush even outshone Blair's with Bush. Even the *cinco mayo* Mexican commemoration of the eviction of the French monarch in the 1860s was celebrated, for the first time, in the White House, while *rancho politics* between the two presidents led many Mexicans to actually believe bilateral relations were being structurally altered for the better. No single issue epitomized these sentiments, and the resultant miscalculations, better than Mexican emigration.[10] By inducing the United States to relax border controls, the Fox-Castañeda team increased the salience of the ever-growing binational population in both Mexican and U.S. politics.[11] This also helped dampen nationalistic resistance to privatizing key public sectors and marketizing agriculture in Mexico.[12] What may be critical is not the expected congressional opposition to any such plan in the United States or how severely it was undermined by 9/11, but the sheer absence of any Mexican alternative. Astute as he was, Castañeda only began to fill the missing blank with Resolution 1441, by which time, for at least three reasons, miscalculation was inevitable: the costs of balancing U.S. interests were too prohibitive for a country as dependent as

Mexico; the benefits of bandwagoning on the United States did not match the loss of Mexican reputation; and the only remaining role for Mexico was to straddle. His New Year's resignation became the dividing line between Fox's activist foreign policy epoch and an uncertain era of reluctant support, indicating a foreign policy bereft of meaningful purpose.[13] Luis Ernesto Derbez, the new foreign secretary, toned down the country's voice, but indecisiveness, for example, in both supporting the UN and appeasing U.S. interests by urging Iraq to comply, reiterated how meaningless the Security Council membership had become.[14] On the Canadian–U.S. front, the two countries share the longest unfortified boundary in the world. That it also witnesses the largest flows of goods and merchandise between any two countries adds to the specialty of the relationship. In the final analysis, both Canada and Mexico are among the top three trading partners of the largest economy in the world today; and the United States alone absorbs over three-quarters or more of the exports of the two neighbours! With 9/11, but more particularly Operation Iraqi Freedom, while many of these long-term trends are unlikely to change significantly, the special status they acquired for both U.S.-based bilateral relationships are expected to dim to some extent. To what extent remains the puzzle, not just for these two countries, but also for the dozens of others for which the United States is the largest market or source of investment funds.

State–Society Disjunctures

Arguments about an overloaded state are not new but assume new meanings in the wake of the stupendous information revolutions underway.[15] With even the most rigid boundaries collapsing, the emerging global village and rapidity of technological innovations only predict greater anomie and further anarchy even in very stable societies.

Three impacts are noteworthy. First, states and societies no longer move in the same direction, and the widening gap between them exacerbates the democratic deficit between policy demands and supplies. Secondly, in turn, especially in emerging democracies, tenures of elected officials may become shorter than before, thus adding to the flux. Finally, just as both of the above dynamics challenge the legitimacy of the domestic order, it is but one short step towards challenging the international order! Behind the ricocheting effects of internal-external reciprocal dynamics stands a more robust version of public opinion than hitherto. It is a critical emerging force in many countries of the world, while in other countries more subtle struggles persist in manipulating it. Whether the media constitute a fourth branch of government or not, they can cast a spell on the public faster than any politicians or most policies and hold both politicians and policies at bay almost as effectively as electoral votes can. How Resolution 1441 exposed the gap between policy positions and public preferences in various countries alerted us to both the power of the latter over foreign policy and the potentially disruptive effects of state-society divergences.

Reciprocating Domestic–External Dynamics

Under the onslaught of boundary-eroding globalization, liberalization, and democratization (GLAD) forces, nationalistic tendencies do not necessarily help. Not only that, but increasing state porosity and transparency also lets the proverbial cat out of the bag, for whatever the results may be!

Mexico's disoriented foreign policy today is an example of the GLAD-induced results. Its hallowed strategy of import substitution was abandoned from the 1980s precisely because global competitiveness had significantly chipped away at Mexican nationalism, isolation, and economic viability. In turn, enormous democratic pressures were released in what the Peruvian poet Mario Llosa Vargas dubbed the *"perfect dictatorship."* Against these forces, like Trudeau's Third Option, Mexico's President Carlos Salinas de Gortari also sought, through his complementation policy in 1989, diversified economic partners in the European Community and Japan to lessen the dependence on the United States. Yet, German unification and the start of Japan's first post-World War II recession thwarted his initiative. His free trade proposal to George Bush Sr. dittoed Mulroney's to Ronald Reagan four years earlier, and for similar reasons. Unpredictable domestic-external intertwinings affect not just Mexico and Canada, but all countries!

Principles versus Pragmatism

Adjusting to the rapidly moving post-Cold War world creates strange bedfellows, not the least between revered principles and ad hoc pragmatism. Mexico's 180-degree turn towards the United States since the 1980s buried the import substitution culture, first institutionalized by Lazáro Cardenás in the 1930s, then reaffirmed by every subsequent president until Miguel de la Madrid in the 1980s. It generated national pride and inflated nationalism. Even by embracing liberalization these deep nationalistic chords are not being tempered. The result is a half-breed circumstance almost every country of the world recognizes in one way or another. It is experienced by *transitional* countries like China, India, or Malaysia, their *developed* counterparts, such as Canada, Japan, or Switzerland, even *underdeveloped* states such as Bangladesh, Nepal, or

Somalia, not to mention today's *outliers*, Afghanistan, Cuba, or North Korea. Routine adjustments are themselves problematic enough, but when they are forced, reactions and a more deteriorating atmosphere seem inevitable.

Conclusions

Trapped as they are between a rock and the United States, countries such as Canada, Mexico, and several others need to reinvent the wheel, if need be, to find an escape route. On the one hand, policymakers under GLAD circumstances must respond to a fair share of public desires, if only to be re-elected. On the other is the desire to profit from the largest economy in human history, and with it all sorts of problems of how to balance domestic welfare considerations or sentimental outbursts with the efficiency imperatives or cutthroat approaches of global competitiveness. The circumstance is an old puzzle fated to continue well into the forseeable future. Two previously tried options remain: diversifying economic partners or accepting vulnerability. Either way, Mexican President Porfírio Díaz's lament at the start of the twentieth century of his country being too far from God and too close to the United States resonates even louder in the twenty-first, not just for Mexico, but also for Canada.

Notes

1   Similar posturings have been widely discussed in the media. On Mexico, for example, see Raúl Benítez Manaut, "Mexico: Dilemmas in the Irak [*sic*]-U.S. conflict," *Voices of Mexico*, no. 62 (Jan.–Mar. 2003): 7–9; Traci Carl, "Mexican president weighs Iraq decision,"

CNews, 12 March 2003, in http://cnews.canoe.ca/CNEWS/World/ 2003/03/12/41654-ap.html; Martin Lloyd, "Security Council: with D.C. waiting, Mexico debates," *The Boston Globe Online*, 3 December, 2003, in http://www.bostonglobe.com/dailyglobe2/071/ nation/With_D_C_waiting_Mexico_debates_vote+...; "Mexico's dilemma," from review of the Mexican press by Jana Schroeder, *World Press Review*, 7 March, 2003, in http://worldpress.org/ Americas/982.cfm; and Nick Miles, "Mexico's Iraq vote dilemma," *BBC News*, 2 March 2003, from http://news.bbc.co.uk/2/hi/ americas/2812795.stm

2   From "Statement of the permanent representative of Mexico to the United Nations, Ambassador Manuel Tello, in the working group on the reform of the Security Council, during the consideration of the question of the veto," http://www.un.int/mexico/discur97/veto-eng.htm

3   On the waning of Cuba in the country's foreign policy firmament, see Roger E. Hernandez, "Mexico and a new Cuba," *News*, 5 April, 2002, 12; and Susan Ferris, "Castro, Fox spar as Mexico 'abandons' Cuba," ibid., 25 April, 2002, 12. This used to be a Mexico City English daily which went out of circulation from 1 January 2003, leaving the city without any daily English newspaper for the moment.

4   A number of incidents fueled this growing great power antagonism: It was Germany's turn to represent Europe in the Security Council; the fortieth anniversary of the Elysees Treaty reaffirmed Franco-German camaraderie; U.S. Secretary of State Colin Powell had just shifted, inexplicably at that, from a diplomatic solution to the Iraq crisis towards outright confrontation; U.S. Defense Secretary Donald Rumsfeld provocatively divided Europe into old and new camps, causing great consternation across Europe; and trumped-up reports villainizing Saddam Hussein's regime by both the United States and Great Britain were not only increasing but were also being challenged for their authenticity! See, among others, Paul Johnson, "French Kiss Off: Lafayette, where are you?" *National Review*, 24 February 2003, 17–18; and "Rumsfeld: France, Germany are 'problems' in Iraqi conflict," CNN, 22 January, 2003, from http://www.cnn.com/2003/WORLD/meast/01/22/sprj.irq.wrap/ index.html

5 On the Mexican proposal, see Frederick W. Mayer, *Interpreting NAFTA: The Science and Art of Political Analysis* (New York: Columbia University Press, 1998), 39–40; and on Canada's, see Gilbert R. Winham, *Trading with Canada: The Canada-U.S. Free Trade Agreement* (New York: Priority Press, 1988). On Canada's initial rejection of Mexican membership, see Andrew F. Cooper, "Canada's Ambivalence: Canada as a Nation of the Americas," Paper presented at the annual convention of the International Studies Association, Chicago, February 1995.

6 Source of the data in this paragraph is his speech itself. See "Notes for an address by prime minister Jean Chrétien to the National Autonomous University of Mexico, February 27, 2003," from pmo@pm.gc.ca

7 PAN lost more than 50 seats in the 500-strong lower house, from the 207 it held to about 155, while the left-wing PRD improved from 56 to 96, and the PRI, which governed Mexico for seventy years until Fox's revolutionary victory in 2002, from 208 to 223, becoming the largest vote-getter by a larger margin. See "Putting the brakes on change," *The Economist*, 12–18 July 2003, 50.

8 Clifford Krauss, "Canadian candidate suggests an effort to mend ties with U.S.," *The New York Times*, 4 May, 2003, from http://www.nytimes.com/2003/05/04/international/americas/04CANA.html?tntemail1, and "Manley's exit, Martin's test," editorial, Toronto Star, 23 July 2003, from http://www.torontostar.com/NASApp/cs/ContentServer?pagename=thestar/Layout/Article_T...p28/07/03

9 See Jack A. Finlayson and Stefano Bertasi, "Evolution of Canadian Postwar International Trade Policy," *Canadian Foreign Policy and International Economic Regimes*, eds. A. Clair Cutler and Mark W. Zacher (Vancouver, BC: British Columbia University Press, 1992), 36–46.

10 For a view untainted by 9/11, see Mónica Verea Campos's "Mexican Migration to the U.S.: Is Regularization Possible?" *Voices of Mexico*, no. 53 (Oct.–Dec. 2000): 69–75.

11 Flavour captured by Anthony York, "Howdy Partner: With Fox Riding High, the Cowboy Summit Showed Mexico is on Top of Bush's List," *MB: The Magazine of the NAFTA Marketplace* 8, no. 1 (July 2000): 14–16; themes reaffirmed by George Bush's first post-

9/11 ambassador to Mexico, in Matthew Brayman, "15 minutes with Tony Garza," *Business Mexico* (February 2003): 8–11.

12 Why agriculture liberalization is thorny is discussed by Pav Jordan, "New NAFTA Phase Seen as Death Blow to Nation's Farmers," *News*, 31 December 2002, 2.

13 Newspaper coverage portrays this vividly. Contrast the upbeat assessment of Mexico's balancing performances prior to the passage of Resolution 1441 with the subdued reports throughout 2003: For the former, see Ioan Grillo, "Mexico's key U.N. Role Applauded by President: Fox: We Had a Lot to Do with the Result," *News*, 9 November 2002, 2; Julia Preston, "Mexico Emerges as Swing Vote at Security Council," ibid., 26 October 2002; 4; "Mexico, France United on Iraq Stance, Fox Says," ibid., 16 November 2002, 2; and Tim Weiner, "Mexico Refuses to Support U.S. Resolution on Iraq," ibid., 28 October 2002, 2. For the latter, see Rodolfo Echeverría Ruiz, "Callejón sin salida," *El Universal*, 7 March 2003, A28; Alejandro Torres Rogelio, "Se mantendrá firme la posición de paz, dice Creel," *El Universal*, 7 March 2003, A14; and Patricia Ruiz, "Vicente Fox reitera a George Bush su postura pacifista," *Milenio Diario*, 7 March 2003, 10.

14 For more, see Alberto Armendáriz, "Proponen a ONU explorar soluciones pacíficas al conflicto: Llama México a Iraq a cumplir con disarme," *Reforma*, 8 March 2003, 2ª.

15 Several articles examine the United States from state, societal, and systemic perspectives in G. John Ikenberry, David A. Lake, and Michael Mastanduno, eds., *The State and American Foreign Economic Policy* (Ithaca, NY: Cornell University Press, 1988); while the strong–weak thesis is propounded and applied by many others in Peter Katzenstein, ed., *Between Power and Plenty: Foreign Economic Policies of Advanced Industrial States* (Madison, WI: University of Wisconsin Press, 1978).

THE MORAL SUPERIORITY COMPLEX IN THE UNITED STATES POSES A MORAL DILEMMA FOR CANADA

Satya R. Pattnayak

The recent U.S.-led war in Iraq and its aftermath have the potential to change the world balance of power in the next few years. Canada as the most important neighbour of the United States faces a moral dilemma. On the one hand, it strives to stabilize and even strengthen the multilateral institutional structure of the United Nations so that world conflicts can be diffused and resolved effectively. On the other hand, however, the Canadian leadership is at pains to see its most important economic partner embark upon a path separate from most members of the UN Security Council. What course of action could Canada possibly have? This chapter contemplates a series of scenarios in which Canada could play a more effective role in the world and hemispheric affairs in the post-war scenario in Iraq.

Canada Faces a Moral Dilemma

The war in Iraq was consistently characterized by the Bush administration as a moral cause. The United States and its allies, as we were told, took a moral stand against a brutal dictator who had defied the UN since the end of Gulf War I in 1991.[1] The official logic was that, unless dealt with immediately, Iraq was likely to use its suspected arsenal of biological, chemical, and possibly nuclear weapons and could strike at the heart of the United States either directly or through surrogates like Osama bin Laden's notorious terrorist organization – al-Qaeda. The British prime minister, Tony Blair, even predicted a scary picture in which Iraq was indeed capable of striking its western enemies with the weapons of mass destruction in a matter of only forty-five minutes. But as a consequence of this "either/or" logic, nations that did not support a pre-emptive military strike against Iraq were demonized not only by key members of the Bush administration but also by the media, in particular the major television networks based in the United States.[2] Of course, the Bush administration probably believed that once the Iraq issue was dealt with in moral terms, then, nations would have to take a stand, and the expectation was that they would support the military campaign.

In order to mobilize a sufficient number of nations behind its military policy in Iraq, or an alliance of the willing, the Bush administration put considerable pressure on many countries, including Canada. It used intimidating language through public announcements by some of the key members of the administration. The characterization of Germany and France as "Old" Europe and being less relevant to the United States contributed to a trans-Atlantic impasse between Washington on the one hand and Berlin and Paris on the other, not seen since the Suez Crisis in 1956. Of all nations that were against the immediate military strike in Iraq, France in particular was subjected to the most embarrassing negative campaign in the United States. Even the speaker of the House, Dennis Hastert, advocated a boycott of French products in the United States. But this was only the tip of the iceberg of a "we don't really need any of them" attitude.

Countries not as economically or politically powerful as Germany and France were subjected to more open political and diplomatic intimidation by members of the Bush administration. In some instances, financial incentives were offered to stand in line behind the U.S. military strike in Iraq, which was subsequently characterized as one intended to liberate the Iraqi people from a cruel and brutal dictatorship.

If a given nation considered important by the U.S. administration did not openly commit itself to stand behind the United States in this simplistic but monstrous battle of biblical proportions between "good" and "evil," then, a significant portion of the media in the United States characterized that country as a "traitor" to the cause of Western civilization.[3] In particular, Canada as the immediate neighbour was put in a really difficult situation. In many ways, the Iraqi problem posed a moral dilemma for Canada.

Based on the newspaper and television coverage in the U.S. of Canada, as limited as it had been, one could say that the public sentiment in Canada was divided to a significant degree. On the one hand, according to some Canadian polls before the war, most "Canadians ... found American foreign policy overtly aggressive and thought American leaders took them for granted."[4] But, on the other hand, "Canadians also thought of themselves as friends of the United States, so at times when anti-Americanism appeared to have been growing, there was always a snap-back reaction. More often than not, Canadian emotions and policies toward the United States were characterized by ambiguity."[5] It was more than just that; it presented a real problem for Canada.

This dilemma was sustained by several hard facts: (1) Canada had had a long-standing commitment to using multilateral forums to resolve international disputes; (2) a long, open border with the United States; (3) an economic partnership that had created the world's two largest trading partners of each other's products; and (4) to people living outside of the North American continent, Canadians, with the exception of Quebec, were not very distinguishable from Americans culturally and linguistically. Of course, Canadians and Americans would dispute this simplistic version of their respective national existence. But the truth is that in order to maintain some semblance of independence from the colossus to the south, successive Canadian governments, although they have cooperated with armed campaigns overseas alongside the United States, at times have done so only grudgingly. In that respect, the recent Canadian cooperation in the campaign against the Taliban and al-Qaeda in Afghanistan in the aftermath of September 11 was noteworthy. Unfortunately, that cooperation also had produced Canadian casualties. Four Canadian soldiers died when they came under fire by mistake from a U.S. National Guard F-16 fighter jet during a training exercise.[6]

The general feeling in some sections in the United States was that, if it could be avoided, Canada would rather use multilateral forums of negotiation and bargaining and not hard military power. In that context, Canada's insistence that the United States use the United Nations in its quest for international legitimacy did not come as a surprise.[7] When that did not materialize, largely due to the intransigence of the U.S. diplomats, Canadian leadership found itself in a difficult situation. In early February of 2003, Prime Minister Jean Chrétien delivered a major speech at the Chicago Council on Foreign Relations in which he had advised that, in spite of U.S. frustrations with the UN, "the long-term interests of the United States would be better served by acting through the United Nations, than by acting alone."[8] In this sense, Canadian preference to act through multilateral organizations such as the United Nations was quite similar to that of Germany and France. The prime minister's speech turned out to be prophetic by the late summer of 2003. Due to sustained hostilities to the U.S. military presence and casualties in Iraq, the American Secretary of State Colin Powell returned to New York to ask for the UN support so that the problems in administering a fragmented Iraq would be minimized. It is to be noted that the same U.S. secretary of state had admonished the UN a few months earlier, when the war talk was heating up in Washington, for not acting on its resolutions aggressively.

Evidence of Hard Power

According to many scholars of the U.S. security policy, this divergence could be explained on the basis of stark differences in hard power.[9] After the end of the Cold War and the realignment of the East Bloc countries, the new Russian Federation was, and remains, neither an economic nor a political challenge to the United States. In addition, the gap between the major NATO countries and the United States also widened, more starkly so since the late 1980s. These vast differences could be explained in terms of the respective perceptions of threat and priorities.[10] While NATO and its European member states focused on creating a European economic powerhouse that would rival the economic dominance of the United States, they had indeed neglected the military component of such power. That disparity has only increased in recent years.[11]

According to the World Bank, the Canadian economy is about 2.2 per cent of the world economy. With 31 million people, the ratio of the size of the economy to the population is 0.071. Compared to this, the U.S. economy is about one-third of the world economy (32.6%) while it caters to a population of 284 million. The corresponding ratio for the United States amounts to 0.115, a much more favourable ratio indicating a more solid base. In plain language, it came down to this:

while the United States possessed 9.2 times the population of Canada, its economy was 14.8 times larger than the Canadian economy.[12] Of course, this asymmetry in hard power becomes much too large to ignore if the preponderance of the U.S. military power is taken into account.

After Gulf War I, the U.S. military spending declined somewhat until 2000, but in the aftermath of 9/11 it increased significantly. Based on the 2003 estimates, the U.S. military spending is now about 40 to 45 per cent of the world military spending.[13] This asymmetry in economic and military power does not end with Canada. The United States also enjoys a disproportionate amount of advantage vis-à-vis Germany and France as well. For example, the economies of Germany and France together constitute about 10.2 per cent of the world economy, which is less than one-third of the U.S. economy. Germany and France cater to a combined population of 141 million. For comparison sake, the U.S. population is about twice the combined population of Germany and France, but its economy is more than three times that of the two economies put together.[14] This power asymmetry is magnified when the military dimension is added. While the NATO economies have been intent on stabilizing or reducing military spending in the aftermath of the demise of the Warsaw Pact, the United States has indeed consolidated and actually augmented its military striking power vis-à-vis the rest of the world combined, commensurate with its unchallenged superpower status.[15] Hence, in U.S. thinking, the military option is likely to be entertained sooner, as only the United States has the capacity to intervene and neutralize threats to its security across this universe, in multiple places simultaneously if necessary. In such a scenario of drastic imbalance of hard power, what could Canada possibly do?

Canada's Place in the Future Balance of Power

Despite its limits in terms of the economic and military power, Canada is no ordinary country for the United States. As stated earlier, it is the biggest trading partner for the United States, but looking at it from the Canadian perspective, the United States imports more than 80 per cent of all Canadian exports, leaving it vulnerable to possible reprisal from Washington. The economic stakes have been ominous in the pronouncements by prominent members of the Canadian political landscape.[16] For example, Canadian Alliance leader Stephen Harper and others had repeatedly asked that Canada should support the American plans for military strikes against Iraq regardless of whether or not it had UN support. These tensions have strong economic undertones. The world's longest open border is also the world's busiest. Despite the dilemma in moral terms, Canadian leaders are aware of the negative economic implications of any protracted disagreement with the United States.

Yet, there are theoretical and, by implication, futuristic limits to the Bush administration's hypothesis that Iraq was a moral problem and that the United States and Britain were on the morally superior side. The reverse logic behind such an hypothesis was that those nations that opposed the 17 March deadline proposed by the Bush administration were immoral by implication, in particular France.

First of all, the demonizing of France and, to a lesser extent, Germany by the Bush administration and the popular media in light of the gridlock in the UN Security Council is only a small problem compared to what might develop in the next three to five years in the form of a competing power bloc, a real counter weight to the United States in the world balance of power.

Since the end of the Cold War, the successive U.S. administrations from Bush I to Clinton to Bush II have created an aura of invincibility around themselves. That aura is sustained by default, meaning that no real competition exists in terms of any worrisome challenge to the U.S. dominance in economic, technological, and military matters. That is at least the perception perpetuated by the hawks in the Bush administration, resulting in an extraordinary amount of arrogance, but not statesmanship and diplomacy. Of course, by comparison with the current Bush administration, the Clintonians look like the nicest people on earth. However, remembering the hawkish posture of the former secretary of state, Madeline Albright, over the war in Serbia, one could make the argument that there has indeed been a greater willingness on the part of the U.S. policy-makers in recent years toward a military solution to a crisis overseas. But that is nothing compared to what might unravel because of an apparent lack of understanding of or patience over the intricacies of international diplomacy.

The temporary spring 2003 alliance of France, Germany, Russia, and China – countries that had opposed the U.S.-British-Spanish proposal in the UN Security Council to wage war in Iraq – could very well become a real, strategic economic, technological, and military alliance. This has an even greater potential as a rival power bloc if Japan joins them in the next few years. Japan has been quite uncomfortable with the current situation in Iraq, and its continued dependence on Mideast oil complicates the issue. Japan has been quietly but seriously in-terested in signing contracts with Russia that, once successful, would build a pipeline from the Russian oil-rich provinces to the eastern ports, and then on to Japan.

Economically, the alliance of France, Germany, Russia, China, and Japan would be as powerful as that of the U.S.-led alliance. Based on the 2002 data, France and these allies would account for about 30 per cent of the world economy while the U.S.-led alliance (U.S.-UK-Spain) would control 39 per cent of the world economy. Technologically, this rival alliance will have the German, French, and the Japanese know-how and, although it may be slightly behind that of the United States in some areas, would be quite at par in electronics, robotics, and communication. Militarily, the United States cannot really threaten the alliance, as Russia still possesses at least as many nuclear weapons as the United States.[17] The Chinese armed forces by most accounts are the largest in the world. This alliance, if it takes shape, would indeed become a competing power bloc in all major dimensions of power – economic, technological, military, and political. With the exception of China, the U.S.-led alliance cannot claim that the competition is between democracy and free market versus totalitarianism and state socialism.

In this possible scenario, Canada could play an effective bridge between the two power blocs, thus becoming more important than at the present for the U.S. policy-makers. With its close political contact with European nations, in particular France and the United Kingdom, this is a likely scenario. The second possible scenario for Canada, although not as glamorous, could be effective as well. Since Canadian refineries process a significant amount of crude oil destined for the U.S. market, it would make prudent sense for the Canadian leadership to work closely with Mexico and Venezuela in the area of oil exploration and distribution. In fact, the recent U.S. Department of Energy data show that Canada, Mexico, and Central and South America together account for more than half of the daily oil imports to the United States.[18] A coordinated platform of Canada, Mexico, and Venezuela together with continued U.S. dependence on foreign oil is bound to accord Canada a greater weight than it currently gets from the United States. Finally, an organized campaign in concert with the various U.S. business houses and chambers of commerce to keep politics out of economics would also be a start. Since the Canadian economy is strongly embedded with the U.S. economy, this option may actually be easier to realize. All of these formations take time, but if played judiciously, Canada would have a more important role to play than at the present in world peace and stability.

As things stand at this critical juncture, there are very few takers of U.S. arrogance internationally. It defies logic when the U.S. administration declares a deadline on Iraq and asks the UN Security Council to vote on it and yet threatens reprisal for non-support. For example, the U.S. ambassador to Mexico hinted at possible reprisals when Mexico could not make up its mind on the U.S.-led proposal.[19] When nations are insulted and are taken for granted, they are likely to organize and make efforts to change the balance of power. That would mean of course that NATO would break up in the next three to five years, and if the current attitude of belligerence continues in the U.S. administration, it will only pave the way for a rival power bloc in the making. And that would spell bad things for the real U.S. national interest. But it could make things more interesting for Canada in a positive way.

In a Post-War Scenario

What is contemplated in the earlier section is theoretical. Scholars writing on the international balance of power among states have consistently predicted the rise of a rival power bloc from an essentially unipolar world, due to a number of game-theory calculations toward gaining economic, political, strategic, and diplomatic advantage over rival states.[20] But there are signs that many of the members of the contemplated rival power bloc are mending fences with the United States. For example, the UN Security Council voted overwhelmingly to recognize the U.S.-imposed Iraqi Governing Council and even agreed to get involved in the post-war reconstruction of Iraq. Canada has already manifested its willingness to work with the United States in the post-war reconstruction efforts. Although these do not include the sending of Canadian soldiers, the Canadian leadership has promised significant help in some key areas. For example, the Canadian prime minister has promised significant help in infrastructure building, humanitarian help, and educating Iraqis in democratic governance.[21]

Both France and Germany are on a "kiss and make up" mode. Both President Chirac of France and Chancellor Schroeder of Germany have been publicly sympathetic toward offering a helping hand in the rebuilding of Iraq. The United States is also facing a rising opposition to the fast-increasing human and financial costs of rebuilding in Iraq. As U.S. soldiers die almost daily in scattered resistance and the cost of maintaining an administration and military presence amount to 4 billion dollars a month, popular opposition is showing signs of emerging. The Democratic Party has also picked up on its opposition to the post-war developments. In this changed scenario, it would also be advantageous for the U.S. administration to get some support from both the UN and its former opponents. In such a situation it is quite easy for Canadian policy makers to forget the long-term repercussions of the U.S.-led war in Iraq without a UN Security Council mandate and, instead, concentrate on the good things Canada shares with the United States, albeit in an asymmetrical fashion.

Without publicly acknowledging it, the U.S. administration has been campaigning for a multilateral military force that would slowly relieve some of the work now being done by the British and American forces. The Central American countries of El Salvador, Honduras, and Nicaragua have recently sent about 900 soldiers to join the military peacekeeping operations in Iraq.²² Soldiers from Georgia, Ukraine and Poland are already on the ground. With the UN resolution now in favour of a multilateral involvement in the reconstruction of Iraq, it is entirely possible that countries such as Jordan, Turkey, Bangladesh, and India could send their military personnel to Iraq to relieve some members of the U.S. forces. It seems there is a grudging acceptance by both sides of the pre-war debate of the new ground realities in post-war Iraq. The post-war Canadian overture to help out the United States in supplying transport aircraft, disaster management assistance, and even hard dollars in the amount of $106 million in Iraq indicates that the larger relevance of the multilateral conflict management through the UN is being compromised by the desire to return to the *status quo antebellum*. The U.S., by turning to the global community for support in re-creating Iraq under its mandate, also acknowledges that its unilateral approach cannot be sustained without serious cost to itself. It would seem that American isolation during the war is coming to an end and that Canada is playing a role in the thaw.

Notes

1 President George W. Bush's televised address to the nation, 17 March 2003, ABC News.

2 The Fox network and the MSNBC have been notorious in this regard, in particular the former.

3 In this regard, talk shows like "O'Reilly Factor" on Fox network are openly hostile to foreign countries that did not wholeheartedly support the U.S. position at the UN Security Council.

4 Clifford Krauss, "Canadians of Two Minds Over Neighbor to the South," *New York Times* (17 March 2003), A10.

5 Ibid., A10.

6 CBC News, taken from http://www.cbc.ca/stories/2002/04/ cdcdeaths020418.

7   http://www.recorder.ca/cp/national/030320/n032099A.html.

8   CBC News, taken from http://www.cbc.ca/stories/2003/02/13/ chretien030213.

9   See Robert Kagan, *Of Paradise and Power* (New York: Alfred A. Knopf, 2003).

10 Samuel P. Huntington, "The Lonely Superpower," *Foreign Affairs* 78 (March/April 1989): 35–49.

11 Wesley K. Clark, *Waging Modern War* (New York: Public Affairs, 2001), 448–49.

12 All calculations are made by the author based on the data provided in The World Bank, *World Development Report 2003* (Washington, DC: The World Bank and Oxford University Press, 2003), 234–39.

13 http://www.fas.org/asmp/fast_facts.htm, 1–8.

14 All calculations are made by the author from data presented in The World Bank, *World Development Report*, 234–39.

15 Thomas L. Pangle and Peter J. Ahrensdorf, *Justice among Nations* (Lawrence: University of Kansas Press, 1999), 200–2.

16 http://www.globeandmail.com/servlet/ArticleNews/front/ RTGAM/20021002/schr1001/fr.

17 Anthony Cordesman, *The Global Military Balance* (Center for Strategic and International Studies, January 2002).

18 www.eia.doe.gov/pub/oil_gas/petroleum/analysis-publications (1996).

19 Evening news coverage, *Channel 2* (Mexico City, 4–5 March 2003).

20 See, for example, Emerson M.S. Niou, Peter C. Ordeshook, and Gregory F. Rose, *The Balance of Power: Stability in International Systems* (New York: Cambridge University Press, 1989).

21 http://cnews.canoe.ca/CNEWS/Canada/200304/29/75736-cp.html.

22 *La Nacion*, San José, Costa Rica, 14 August 2003, 25–28.

FOREIGN AND DEFENCE POLICY INDEPENDENCE: WILL THIS BE OUR VERY LAST CHANCE?

Mel Hurtig

The Chrétien government's decision not to join the American invasion of Iraq surprised and pleased most Canadians. Since the invasion, public opinion polls have consistently shown the majority of Canadians supported the government's decision and in recent months that support has grown even stronger. Here and elsewhere the invasion is increasingly seen as an illegal and tragic imperialistic blunder, which is well on the way to producing a Vietnam-like quagmire while generating widespread hatred and increasing terrorism around the world, with more and worse certain to come in the future.

The pressure on the Chrétien government to join George W. Bush's ill-advised "pre-emptive" aggression was unrelenting. The threats from the likes of U.S. ambassadors Paul Cellucci and Gordon Giffin and Condoleezza Rice were blunt and arrogant. Canada was expected to join in and it would be "unthinkable" if we did not. *Time* magazine said, "Canada could play a hefty price for the government's anti-war stance." Meanwhile, our own plutocratic Americanizers were vociferous in their support for Bush, Rumsfeld and the Pentagon. Most of our press weren't far behind. A *Globe and Mail* columnist wrote, "Simply put, if we get too far from the Americans, we get punished." Continentalist historian Jack Granatstein said that Canada has "no choice" but to co-operate fully with the United States. Stephen Harper and the Official Opposition were strongly in favour of going to war. So was virtually all of the powerful and influential big-business community in Canada – much of it foreign-owned and controlled.

Over and over, Canadians were warned about our vulnerability if we chose not to go to war. Our exports would be threatened; the border would be closed; further planned and anticipated integration in the form of "The Big Idea" and "The Grand Bargain" would be in danger. Our standard of living would be sure to plummet. What was so remarkable about the Chrétien decision was that, since its election in 1993, the government had been the most continentalist, conservative Liberal government in modern Canadian history. With so many staunch American sycophants in the cabinet and on the backbenches, and with a foreign affairs department that long ago forgot the meaning of words like "sovereignty," "independence" and "self-respect," it seemed that most likely "ready, aye ready!" would be the Canadian response. Is there much doubt that that would indeed have been the Canadian response if Jean Chrétien were not entering the last months of his reign as prime minister? I think not. Is there any doubt about what Paul Martin would have done? Once again I think not.

The public opinion polls continue to be revealing (despite some silly headlines in the *National Post*). Most Canadians want us to be independent of American domination, want us to support multilateralism, want us to preserve our own standards, values and quality of life. Yet, whatever pride we can take in relation to our principled decision regarding Iraq, will be quickly trampled by a Paul Martin government's uncompromising rush to join Bush's National Missile Defence (NMD) plan, to integrate our military with the U.S. military, to place us behind the North American Security Perimeter, while selling off even more of the ownership and control of our country. Anyone who is familiar with Bush's new Star Wars plan knows that it will result in the weaponizing of space, the de-stabilization of arms agreements, the proliferation of nuclear weapons, the rapid development of more powerful nuclear weapons, and improved multiple-warhead missile delivery systems. For Canada to adopt a fawning, obsequious behaviour in the face of such potential disaster will certainly end our ability to ever again demonstrate foreign and defence policy independence.

What agreements that Canada supports and in some cases helped initiate will have to be abandoned because the United States doesn't like them? Will it be the Land Mines Treaty? The International Criminal Court? The Small Arms Treaty? The UN Protocol on Developing, Producing or Stockpiling Biological or Toxic Weapons, or a long list of other international agreements the rogue Bush administration detests? If Canada abandons its long-standing opposition to the weaponizing of space by supporting the NMD, and if we further integrate our military with the U.S. military, any proud remnant of our foreign policy legacy will be swept down the drain forever. Paul Martin is a strong supporter of the WTO Doha Round, the FTAA, the GATT, the World Bank, and the International Monetary Fund, all with their mantras of privatization, deregulation, and the "free flow of capital" (the euphemism for selling off the ownership and control of our country that is not already foreign-controlled).

A Canadian Council on National Unity poll has shown that two-thirds of Canadians say that maintaining the sovereignty of Canada is *the* most important challenge facing our country, while only 8 per cent want us to become more like the United States, and three in five say that we are losing our independence from the United States. A full 89 per cent say that the quality of life is better in Canada than it is in the United States. Yet, with the Paul Martin government, we're going to be rapidly heading to even more integration, more harmonization, and more Americanizied policies, standards, and values.

Timid Canadian continentalists (and there are many of them in the federal government and in our business community) claim that we are so vulnerable to the United States that we really *must* toe the American line, or else. This is nonsense. Fifty-four per cent of our entire trade surplus with the United States comes from our exports of oil, natural gas, and electricity. We supply 99 per cent of U.S. electricity imports, 94 per cent of their natural gas imports, 17 per cent of oil, and 35 per cent of their uranium used for power generation. To suggest that these exports are in any way vulnerable is absurd. Then, if you subtract the huge annual U.S. surplus in services, which are mostly imports into Canada by American branch plants from their parent companies at inflated and very profitable non-arm's-length prices, and then subtract the huge $30 billion-plus annual U.S. investment income surplus with Canada, our overall net surplus with the United States shrinks to well under 1 per cent of GDP. Consider, too, that Canada is the number one customer of U.S. corporations and has been for the past forty-eight consecutive years. We buy more goods and services from the United States than all fifteen European Union countries combined. U.S. exports to Canada, plus their investment income from Canada, exceed their income from any other country by an enormous $177 billion!

A proud, independent, self-confident Canada should be playing a much greater role in the United Nations, should be joining the post-Cancun group of nations (China, India, Brazil, etc.) to counter the WTO establishment vision of corporate globalization, should quickly step up its foreign aid, should strongly support multilateral agreements to promote peace and disarmament, and should reject imperialism in all its forms – and say so without reservation. We can't do any of these things unless we stop the growth of the foreign ownership and control of our country. A colony doesn't have an independent foreign or defence policy. A colony's young men and women go off to fight imperial wars, be it in the Middle East or in North Korea, or where have you.

Those of us who love our country, value our freedom to chart our own future, and have children and grandchildren that we want to grow up to be Canadian must do much more in the future if our wonderful country, so full of promise and opportunity, is to survive for our future generations. And what a shining example we could be for other democracies. And what a tragedy it would be if we fail.

Notes on Contributors

Colleen Beaumier is the Liberal M.P. for Brampton-West Mississauga. Prior to the U.S. invasion, she visited Iraq on a fact-finding trip to study the effects of UN sanctions on the population.

Dr. Arthur Clark is a citizen of the United States and of Canada and served as a Captain in the U.S. Army Medical Corps, 1971–73. Currently a professor in the Faculty of Medicine at the University of Calgary, he helped establish the Dr. Irma Parhad programmes at the University of Calgary, which are concerned with conditions influencing human health and well-being worldwide.

Trudy Govier, PhD, is a philosopher, who lives and works in Calgary. A longtime member of Project Ploughshares, Dr. Govier is the author of a number of philosophical works, including *A Practical Study of Argument, Social Trust and Human Communities*, and *A Delicate Balance: What Philosophy Can Tell Us about Terrorism*.

Robert Hackett, PhD, is a professor in the School of Communication at Simon Fraser University. He co-directed NewsWatch Canada from 1993 to 2003. His books include *Sustaining Democracy? Journalism and the Politics of Objectivity, The Missing News: Filters and Blind Spots in Canada's Press*, and *Political Communication and the News Media in Democracies: Competing Perspectives*.

Jim Harding, PhD, is adjunct professor of human justice at the University of Regina. He has been active in the peace movement since the Ban-the-Bomb campaign in the 1950s. Among his books are *Social Policy and Social Justice* and *Nuclear Politics* *in Saskatchewan* (forthcoming). Now semi-retired, he gardens organically in Saskatchewan's Qu'Appelle Valley and works on the Crows Nest Ecology Preserve. His book, *After Iraq: War, Imperialism and Democracy* is forthcoming in 2004.

Mel Hurtig is an Officer of the Order of Canada and the recipient of six honorary degrees. He has been the National Chairman of the Committee for an Independent Canada and is the founder and former Chairman of the Council of Canadians. He is the author of *The Betrayal of Canada*, *Pay the Rent or Feed the Kids*, and his autobiography *At Twilight in the Country*. His most recent book is *The Vanishing Country: Is It Too Late to Save Canada?*

Imtiaz Hussain, PhD, is professor in the Department of International Studies, Universidad Iberoamericana (Mexico City). Dr. Hussain's interests include NAFTA dispute-settlement processes, comparative regionalization, and trade security issues. He is a native of Bangladesh, who holds a doctorate in political science from the University of Pennsylvania.

Jacqueline S. Ismael, PhD, is professor of social work at the University of Calgary. She is author, co-author and/or editor of over ten books on social policy and social development. Her latest works include *The Oppressive State in the Arab World* (2001) and the forthcoming (with Tareq Ismael) *The Iraqi Predicament: People in the Quagmire of Power Politics*.

Tareq Y. Ismael, PhD, is professor of political science, University of Calgary. He is the author, co-author or editor of twenty-one books on the Middle East. His most recent works are *The International Relations of the Middle East in the 21st Century: Patterns of Continuity and Change* (2000), *Middle*

East Politics Today: Government and Civil Society (2001), and *Iraq: The Cost of History* (2003).

Donn Lovett is a Calgary peace activist who has been to Iraq on several occasions.

George Melnyk is assistant professor of Canadian Studies in the Faculty of Communication and Culture at the University of Calgary. He is the author of numerous books on Canadian society. Most recently he co-edited *Canada and September 11: Impact and Response* (2002).

Joyce Patel, M.A., is a research assistant in Colleen Beaumier's Parliament Hill office.

Satya R. Pattnayk, PhD, is associate professor of sociology and director of Latin American studies at Villanova University. His most recent book is *Economic Performance under Democratic Regimes in Latin American in the Twenty-First Century.*

The Very Reverend Bill Phipps is a former Moderator of the United Church of Canada. He serves as an International President of the World Conference of Religions for Peace. He is currently Minister of Scarboro United Church in Calgary.

Scott Ritter is the former UN Chief Weapons Inspector in Iraq and a former U.S. Marine. He served with UNSCOM from 1991 to 1998. He is the author of *Endgame: Solving the Iraq Crisis* and collaborated on *War with Iraq: What Team Bush Doesn't Want you to Know.*

Douglas Roche is an author, parliamentarian and diplomat. He served as Canada's Ambassador for Disarmament from 1984 to 1989. He was elected to four terms as Member of